Y0-BCS-046

The 7 Best Practices For Teaching Teenagers The Bible

Published by youth**ministry**360 in the United States of America.

ISBN 13: 9781935832201
ISBN 10: 1935832204

Design and Layout: Upper Air Creative
Copy Editor: Lynn Groom

All quotations taken from *THE COMPLETE GATHERED GOLD, A treasury of quotations for Christians*. John Blanchard, ed. Evangelical Press, 2006.

The 7 Best Practices for Teaching Teenagers the Bible

BY: ANDY BLANKS

Published by youth**ministry**360

SETTING THE STAGE

I have worked over the Bible, prayed over the Bible for more than sixty years, and I tell you there is no book like the Bible. It is a miracle of literature, a perennial spring of wisdom, a wonderful book of surprises, a revelation of mystery, an infallible guide of conduct, an unspeakable source of comfort.—**Samuel Chadwick**

It is not the man who brings the Word that saves the soul, but the Word which the man brings.—**Thomas Arthur**

Do your best to present yourself to God as one approved, a workman who does not need to be ashamed and who correctly handles the word of truth.
—2 Timothy 2:15

TABLE OF CONTENTS

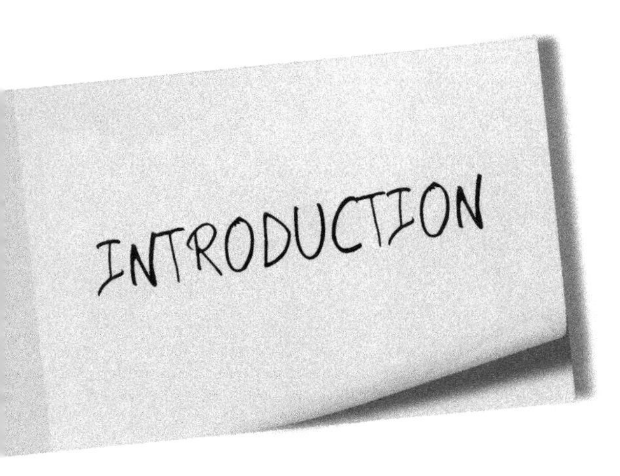

Mr. Masquelier was my hero because he did what so many others had failed to do. Let me explain . . .

Like you, I've had countless teachers in my life, taking me through course after course of life's "need-to-knows." In every subject, the material before me held great potential. In every class, there was always *something* in the curriculum that was noteworthy, or important. Much of it, I was told, came from the greatest minds that ever lived. Einstein. Shakespeare. Newton, and so on . . .

Yet in all of those classes, I never grasped the value of what was waiting for me in my textbooks.

While I was diligently focused on coming up with the right answers, finishing my assignments, and passing all my tests, I'm not sure I ever really thought about the idea that I was supposed to actually be learning something! In so many of these classes, I never really came close to actually discovering the "hidden" knowledge that was right in front of me . . .

Until Mr. Masquelier came along.

Mr. Masquelier taught my least favorite subject: English. I dreaded English class, especially Mr. Masquelier's Sophomore English course. On the first day, I read the syllabus and quickly realized this class would require more of me than any English class before it. I dreaded the thought of all the work that was to come. You see, I knew all about textbooks and their boring facts. What I didn't know about was how big an impact the right teacher could have.

Mr. Masquelier changed everything for me. The books I had always looked at with such apathy suddenly came to life! For the first time, they actually meant something to me. Mr. Masquelier not only made learning stick, he squeezed the very best out of me! Under Mr. Masquelier, I wrote reports, aced tests, and flew through projects with a passion for learning that had previously been untapped. (If only my science teachers could have seen me.)

Mr. Masquelier made the material matter. It mattered so much that before I really even knew it, my attitude about learning and about school was changing. I looked forward to every class Mr. Masquelier offered in high school. Why? Because when I was in his class, I was at my best.

I believe that those of us who are privileged enough to teach the Bible to teenagers posses the same potential for impact that Mr. Masquelier lived out in his classroom.

Of all the texts that have been collected throughout history, the words of Scripture stand alone. They are by far the most powerful and transforming words ever penned. And by teaching these words, we get the chance to step into our student's worlds, grab their hearts and minds, and carry them on a gripping journey. We go beyond mere facts as we lead them to the Well and offer them a drink of living water. This is an amazing privilege, one that should make us both excited and a little in awe.

On the following pages, Andy Blanks helps set you up for success on this journey by offering tools and tips that will draw the best out of you and your teaching. From years of study and experience, Andy will first take you past the distractions and obstacles of everyday youth ministry to spend some time studying your students from a Kingdom view. This will unveil how the spider web of students' experiences, passions, and expectations can all be utilized to squeeze the best out of them when fueled by a Kingdom perspective and most importantly, the King, Himself.

Andy does a great job of showing us practical, life-giving ways we can refine our teaching skills, and continue to make disciples. You're going to love this book!

Doug Franklin
Founder, LeaderTreks

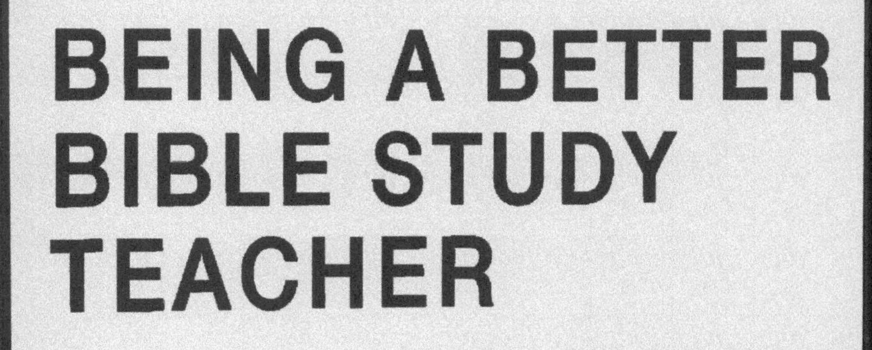
BEING A BETTER
BIBLE STUDY
TEACHER
34 Street–Herald Sq
Station
B D F V
N Q R W
Elevator on B'way
between 33 & 34 Sts

Philosophy and religion may reform, but only the Bible can transform.—**Brian H. Edwards**

For the word of God is living and active. Sharper than any double-edged sword, it penetrates even to dividing soul and spirit, joints and marrow; it judges the thoughts and attitudes of the heart. — Hebrews 4:12

There are skills I'm pretty good at. I can handle myself pretty well in a workshop. I'm no craftsman by any means, but I can refinish furniture, sling drywall mud, or build furniture with the best of them. I've built houses before. In this particular discipline, and maybe one or two more, I'm fairly adept. Better than average.

There are other skills I'm OK at. I'm an OK cook. I'm an OK photographer. I'm an OK fantasy baseball player. (So maybe a little less than OK on that one, but a man can dream, can't he?) I have a passable level of ability at quite a few skills or concentrations.

There are a whole host of skills at which I pretty much stink. I know how to play guitar, but I'm awful. I'm absolutely terrible at golf. Seriously. It's not pretty. I can't dance. I can't act. And I can't sing.

Now here's an interesting thought. What if I wanted to be a better golfer? I could be, couldn't I? I could take lessons, invest in clubs, practice my swing on the driving range, and begin to gain experience through playing regularly. I could improve. But I don't. And I won't. You want to know why?

There are well-meaning, good-hearted men and women all across this country who are not very good Bible teachers, and who have never made the effort to improve.

I couldn't care less if I'm a good golfer or not.

Being good at golf is not a value I hold. It's not important to me to be proficient at hitting the links. And because this is true, I will probably never invest the time and energy it takes to become good at it. Golfing isn't something I'm going to do on a regular basis. It would be futile for me to play very much golf considering I'm a bad golfer and I haven't really done the work to become a better one.

And yet, there are well-meaning, good-hearted men and women all across this country who are not very good Bible teachers, and who have never made the effort to improve. And yet they still teach the Bible each Sunday.

Why aren't they seeking to be better Bible teachers? Certainly there are many factors that may play into this. But at its core, it's an issue of importance. For many people, being a more dynamic Bible teacher is just not something they value.

Now, I want to be quick to say that I'm not in any way disparaging these people. Not one bit. I love these folks! The adult volunteer who works a day job and teaches teenagers in Sunday School or small groups is my kind of person. My belief is simply that the vast majority of these people have no idea they aren't good Bible teachers. They love teenagers, they feel called to serve, and they are teaching the way they were taught. So, I'm not critical. I'm compassionate.

The purpose of this book is two-fold. The primary purpose is definitely that you would become a better teacher of the Bible. My prayer is that this book will help you be a better Bible teacher by giving you some extremely practical and easy-to-implement strategies. This book will help you teach the Bible better.

But more than this, the purpose of this book is to help you remember, or see for the first time, the value of being a great Bible teacher.

WHY WE DO WHAT WE DO

Before we get into the practical stuff, I want to ask you a question . . .

What drove you to pick up this book?

What was it that moved you to open the cover and flip through the first few pages? What caused you to browse an online bookstore and go through the process of downloading this to your e-reader of choice? My hunch is that the reason you're currently reading this book is the same reason I sat down to write it. I'm willing to bet that you're compelled not by obligation, but by desire.

And I bet you're not entirely driven by the desire to be excellent at the skill of teaching the Bible. I bet you're motivated by something deeper. You see, this is where my golf analogy falls flat. While being a better Bible teacher is in many ways about skill development, unlike improving at golf, there's more than proficiency motivating your desire to teach the Bible better.

If you teach the Bible to teenagers on a regular basis, there is something inside you that believes this is a worthy pursuit. Like me, you want to see teenagers live vibrant, dynamic faith lives. You and I are passionate about seeing teenagers know God more. We lead students closer to God. And we primarily do this through teaching them about God through the Bible.

We teach them on Sunday mornings in a large classroom.

Or on weeknights in small groups in somebody's home.

Or maybe on a Sunday night at a coffee shop.

Whatever it looks like, you are in some ways responsible for standing in front of students and leading, or facilitating, or teaching them. But what we teach them is what this book is all about.

HOW WE DO WHAT WE DO

So what do we teach students? Well, we're not teaching students to be better at math. We're not teaching them government, or economics, or chemistry. We're leading students deeper in their relationship with Christ. And we need to get on the same page about how we do this.

The primary way God has made Himself known to His children is through the Bible. I've written about this extensively so forgive any redundancy. But it's a subject I'm really quite passionate about. Why? Because if we're not careful, we can make youth ministry about a lot of different things. We can get caught up in building our efforts on a lot of different platforms that, if not framed in the right light, can actually disctract us from the very things they are intended to point to.

We can build our ministries on relationships.
We can build our ministries on service.
We can build our ministries on worship.
We can build our ministries on evangelism.

When we build our ministries on one or any combination of these pursuits, we're not far off. Each of these is an important aspect to the faith lives of teenage Christ-followers. But if we fail to ground students in the truths of the Bible, then we fail to put any of these things in proper context.

For relationship, service, worship, and evangelism to be realized as God would have them realized, they have to be understood in the context of God's character and in His Kingdom principles. If our relationships with our students don't start with an understanding of our identities as God's children, they're no different that their relationships with their agnostic, Muslim, or Hindu friends. Outside of a right understanding of God and His ways, our worship becomes feel-good emotionalism that serves to meet a need in us, but that is certainly not directed at God. Apart from God's Kingdom principles that are communicated only through His Word, our service becomes nothing but mere volunteerism.

For relationship, service, worship, and evangelism to be realized as God would have them be realized, they have to be understood in the context of God's character and in His Kingdom principles.

If our relationships with students are to produce more fully committed followers of Christ, they must be built on the full knowledge of God Himself. This simply cannot happen without a solid understanding and application of the Bible. Again, this is the very reason God gave us the Bible! So that we might know Him. Sure, there are aspects of God that are mysterious and unknowable (thankfully!). But His character, His history of working in the world and in humankind, His attributes, His unfailing desire to redeem us, His expectations for us as His children, His glorious plan for the future. . . . All of these things can be known! And they are known through the Bible.

If this is true, and I believe it is or I wouldn't be writing this book, then it's pretty important that we know the Bible, and that we know how to teach it in such a way that it's real, relevant, responsible, and that leads to life change. We can offer our students nothing less! And, in all reality, we can offer God nothing less.

So, that's my appeal to you. That's my pitch, so to speak. As people who are motivated by our love for God and by our desire to see students have an active faith that influences their lives, we need to know how to teach the Bible better. Not for the sake of being good Bible teachers. But for the sake of being obedient to Christ's command to make disciples.

WHAT WE'RE NOT DOING

Before we move on, I want to take a second and acknowledge two points of potential contention, lest you or I become tempted to travel down either of these roads.

Point 1: There are well-meaning people whose zeal for the Bible has replaced a zeal for God Himself.

One of my favorite artists is Michael Gungor. He alludes to this issue in the very excellent song "Cannot Keep You":

"We cannot keep you in a church.
We cannot keep you in a Bible,
Or it's just another idol to box you in."

I get it. I understand if you have a sensitivity to this based on past experiences with someone who has this bent. When our love for the security that comes with knowledge and rules replaces the love for the security we have in God, something is wrong. We've missed it.

I hope that you've picked up from this introduction my belief that spiritual transformation is ultimately found in and through Christ. *My contention is simply that God gave us the Bible so that we can have authentic encounters with Him on a regular basis.* Being a better Bible teacher creates more and truer spiritual moments for the students you teach.

Point 2: While we can seek to be the best teachers of the Bible we can possibly be, we can't minimize the role of the Holy Spirit, or the uniquely supernatural role of the Bible itself, in leading students in transformation.

The Spirit ultimately ushers and empowers spiritual formation. But when you do an awesome job of teaching the Bible, you create some seriously fertile ground for the Spirit to work. You become a vessel for the Spirit, not a hindrance.

WRAPPING UP

In wrapping up this introduction, please hear me say that my purpose for this book is to equip you to help your students see God and be radically moved by Him. The ideas in this book represent only a few of the methods of doing this. There are certainly other strategies out there. I humbly offer the suggestions contained in this book with a simple hope: that you might become more intentional about how you teach the Bible. If I can help you lean even the slightest bit in this direction, my time will have been well spent.

As the title suggests, this book will look at a few of the "best practices" of Bible teaching. These aren't prescriptions as much as they are suggestions. The goal is for you to capture the essence of them and to make them your own. We'll spend one chapter on each of them. The seven best practices of teaching the Bible are:

Best Practice #1: Engaging With God
Best Practice #2: Prepare Well, Teach Well
Best Practice #3: Context Is Key
Best Practice #4: Embrace Unpredictability
Best Practice #5: Plan For Interaction
Best Practice #6: Teach For Application
Best Practice #7: Know Your Role

ONE LAST THING

Let me say one last thing before we jump in . . .

I think you're awesome. Seriously.

I know, I know. . . . I may not actually know you, but if you're someone who invests his or her life in leading students to grow in their faith, then I think you're flat-out incredible. I mean it.

I often hear people say that youth ministry is in a sad state, or our churches stink, or that teenagers are abandoning their faith, and so on. Here's what I know: As long as there are men and women like you sharing their lives with teenagers, there's a tremendous hope for the future.

I also know your time is a valuable commodity. Thank you for giving it to this book. Prayerfully, my efforts have made it worth your while. Now let's get to it.

BEST
PRACTICE
#1:
ENGAGING
WITH GOD

Ignorance of the Scripture is ignorance of Christ.—**Jerome**

"You diligently study the scriptures because you think that by them you possess eternal life. These are the scriptures that testify about me." — John 5:39

I want you to put on your imagination cap with me. What's an imagination cap, you ask? Well, it's kind of like a thinking cap, but you're not thinking. You're imagining. Get it? Ridiculous, I know . . . But, humor me . . .

Imagine you and I find ourselves stranded in a car with an engine that's stopped running. Now imagine that I'm going to lead you to repair the engine so that we can get our car moving once again.

I'm imagining it with you. And in my mind, the conversation is going something like this:

ME: *[Opening hood. Hands on hips. Staring intently, but silently. Nodding ever so slightly.]*

YOU: *[Looking at engine. Looking at me. Looking back at engine. Now back at me. You sigh.]* So . . .

ME: *[Hands still on hips. Still staring.]* Yes. So . . .

YOU: *[Just staring at me.]* So, you think you know what's wrong?

ME: *[Clearing throat. Intense staring.]* Well, yeah. . . . I mean, no. Not exactly. But, yes. I mean, there's a lot that could potentially be going wrong, you know? It could be the, uh, [frantically trying to recall names of engine parts] the manifold. Or the calipers. Or of course, the belts. Or the hoses. Belts or hoses.

YOU: *[Picking up tool box]* Well, we should probably try to get it fixed. Where should we start?

ME: Uh, well, uh *[shaking head, confused]*, you could grab that wrench and see about checking on some of the uh, the parts. You know *[scrunching up face]* make sure they're fastened. Connected! Make sure the connections are all connected . . . [mumbling].

YOU: *[Dropping tool box.]* I'm walking.

While this conversation is entirely fictional, it's not far off base. If I were tasked with teaching you or anyone else how to diagnose and repair a problem with an engine, it wouldn't go well. And the reason for this isn't that complicated.

I don't know how to fix an engine, and I can't teach what I don't know.

(See where I'm headed here?)

As individuals tasked with teaching students the Bible, we have to know what it is we're teaching. We need more than a basic understanding of the Bible if we hope to equip others to understand it. We have to wear a faith that has been shaped by our own interaction with God through His Word. After all, your main reason for teaching the Bible isn't so that students know how to better study it.

That's right. I just said that your main purpose in teaching teenagers the Bible is not to teach them better methods of studying its concepts. I know this flies in the face of much of what you hear people say when they talk about teenagers and the Bible. But your main purpose isn't to help students build a treasure chest of memory verses. Your main task isn't to teach the Bible's various facts, or details. Is this information important? Of course. But the primary reason you teach the Bible isn't to build more efficient information collectors. If you think about it, your main purpose for teaching the Bible is actually a whole lot more important than skill development.

The main reason you teach the Bible is to see teenagers' lives transformed.

The main reason you teach the Bible is to see teenagers' lives transformed. You're primarily interested in spiritual growth. You teach the Bible so students will know God and grow in their imitation of Him. You're in the "desire feeding" business. The Spirit helps spur on the desire to know God, and you help feed that desire through facilitating meaningful times of Bible study where Scripture reveals God and His ways.

I wrote earlier that you can't teach what you don't know. Maybe I should have said:

You can't lead students to desire that which you don't desire.

You can't teach students to hunger after that which you don't hunger for.

You can't encourage a spark for closeness with God if you haven't kindled a fire within yourself.

PUT SIMPLY, BEST PRACTICE #1 IS THIS:

> To be an effective Bible teacher, you must regularly seek to know God by engaging with Him through His Word.

A word of warning: The remainder of this chapter is very different than the ones that will follow it. It's a little longer. And it's a lot less practical in terms of giving you a lot of "hooks" to hang your "awesome Bible teacher" hat on. I promise you that in the rest of this book we'll concern ourselves with methodology, strategies, tips, and practical application. But this chapter is kind of like a doctor's visit. (Don't everyone stand up and cheer at once.) Before we can look at treatments, we have to be on the same page about our diagnosis. We have to make sure you and I are both identifying the same illness as the root of the symptoms that need addressing.

I think there is indeed an illness that plagues the Church in general and youth workers specifically. I believe very strongly that we have lost much of our personal hunger for God, a God who is most fully encountered through the Bible.

I want to take the next few pages to meet this illness head on. I want you and me to deal with this issue with an eye toward coming up with a solution.

Can I ask you a favor? Would you resist those urges you're feeling right now to skip ahead or tune me out?

Instead, let's take just a little bit of time to evaluate where you are in your personal study of the Bible.

GETTING PERSONAL

How is your spiritual growth? If you're like a lot of youth workers, you might not be exactly where you want to be. Most of you know who Josh Griffin is. Josh is the High School Pastor at Saddleback and is the lead voice on the excellent blog, MoreThanDodgeball.com. In December 2010, Josh ran a simple poll on his blog[1]. The question? "How has your devotional Bible reading been the past 30 days?" Josh wanted to know how well his audience was personally seeking God through His Word. Josh got a nice response: 443 people. Out of those 443 people, here's the breakdown by percentage of how their Bible reading time had gone over the prior 30 days:

- **Solid**—18.71%
- **OK**—34.41%
- **Hurting a little**—38.34%
- **Zero**—8.55%

While you can't view this poll as truly representative of all youth workers, it does give us a visual picture that I think would probably hold true across an even greater number of respondents. And the picture isn't that great:

- Less than 1 in 5 youth workers said they had a "solid" month of personal time engaging with God through His Word.
- Nearly 3 out of 4 youth workers described their efforts as "OK" or "hurting."
- Nearly 1 in 10 youth workers reported they hadn't had a personal time with God at all in the previous month.

This isn't the general population. This is youth workers! People like you and me who are deeply invested in the spiritual growth of teen-agers. And 46 percent of them stated that their time seeking God in the Bible was either hurting or zero. Ouch!

[1] http://www.morethandodgeball.com/youth-ministry/poll-day-reading-the-bible.html. Accessed February 3, 2012.

So, look back at Josh's poll responses and ask yourself: Where am I on this spectrum? Stop for a second and take your own evaluation of your biblical habits. Where do you fall over the last month? What about the last year? I'll admit, there are months for me that have been "solid," and months that have been "hurting a little." I bet you would report the same thing.

Let's go a step further. Let's take a moment to evaluate your attitude and behavior surrounding the personal time you spend reading and studying your Bible. Take a minute or so to answer this simple series of questions to get a feel for your current relationship with God and your Bible.

[Hey! Where are you going? Why are you breezing pass this section? You don't have two minutes to reflect on where you stand in your desire to grow closer to God? I'm not being pushy, but maybe the fact that you were not about to participate in this activity tells you all you need to know about your current level of engagement with the Bible. OK, so maybe that was pushy, but it's more tough love than anything!

I'll tell you what I tell my students: You have a chance, right now, to make a change, to do something about where you are. God has led you to this point. But you have to act on it. Slow down, clear your head, and take a second to answer these questions, really thinking about the picture your responses paint.]

1. **How many times in the last week did you read your Bible?**
   - ❑ 4-5 times
   - ❑ 2-3 times
   - ❑ 1 time
   - ❑ 0 times

2. **Think before you answer: What real impact do the teachings of the Bible have on your everyday decisions and view of the world?**
   - ❑ God's teachings from the Bible shape my daily attitude, outlook, and decisions.

- ❑ I wouldn't say the Bible influences all of these aspects of my daily life, but it's important to me.
- ❑ Occasionally I'll make a decision based on the Bible.
- ❑ The Bible really has very little impact on my daily life.

3. Describe your comfort level with answering unscripted questions from students about the Bible.

- ❑ No worries. Bring on the questions!
- ❑ Not too uncomfortable, but not real crazy about it either.
- ❑ I get pretty nervous when hands go up.
- ❑ Terrified. I lose sleep before I teach over it.

4. Be honest with yourself: When you think about spending time engaging with God through Bible Study, what emotional reaction do you have?

- ❑ Very positive. I get excited when I think about finding God in and through the Bible.
- ❑ Somewhat positive. In general, I enjoy Bible study.
- ❑ Not very positive. I struggle with consistently getting "up" for Bible study.
- ❑ Negative. If I'm honest with God and myself, I really don't enjoy studying my Bible.

5. How well do you know God? In the margin of your printed book, on a sheet of scrap paper, or on the notes app of this e-reader, jot down as many attributes or characteristics of God as you can. (For example, one attribute of God is "loving.") How many were you able to jot down?

- ❑ 12 or more
- ❑ 8-11
- ❑ 4-7
- ❑ 0-3

6. When life gets you down, or you find yourself in the midst of a trial, what role does the Bible play in providing you with hope or comfort?

- ❑ Plays a huge role. I am strengthened by God and His ways as I see Him at work through the Bible.

- ❑ I find some comfort in the Bible. I generally feel better after reading the Bible during tough times.
- ❑ The Bible doesn't play a big role in comforting me in times of trouble.
- ❑ I find no real comfort in Scripture when things get tough.

7. How willing are you to dialogue with others (friends and strangers) over biblical themes and issues?

- ❑ I'll have those discussions with anyone, anytime.
- ❑ I'll occasionally enter into discussions about what I'm learning in the Bible.
- ❑ I don't do it often, but I have before.
- ❑ I intentionally avoid discussions about biblical themes and issues.

Now, this is by no means scientific. The number of times you read your Bible last week doesn't have a measurable effect on your relationship with God. But, it can serve to show you where your heart is. You might be unwilling to talk with people about biblical issues because you have *lalophobia* and are afraid to talk to anyone about anything, much less the Bible. But, more than likely, this question may be a sign that your fear of discussing biblical issues is based on the fact that you don't know God or His Word as well as you should.

The goal of this little exercise isn't to shame you or guilt you into turning toward God. That's not a healthy mindset in which to approach a relationship with God or with the Bible. And it's certainly not how God wants us to view Him or His Word. The goal of the questions was to get you thinking about your current level of desire for God as He is "encounter-able" through the Bible.

The important question is, what now? What are you going to do about it? If Best Practice #1 is to regularly seek to know God by engaging with Him through His Word, and you're feeling that you could use a little help with that, what are some practical ways you could go about it? Great question.

STRATEGIES FOR CREATING A DESIRE TO SEEK GOD

Here are three general ways of thinking about the strategy of growing your desire for seeking God through His Word.

The Best Way To Cultivate A Hunger For Reading The Bible Is To Read The Bible

The Bible is unlike any other book in two important ways. One, it's "living and active," according to Hebrews 4:12. **What does this mean?** It means the words of God aren't just ink on paper. God's Word is an agent of change in our lives. I love the way the normally erudite *Expositor's Bible Commentary* (EBC) addresses this verse. Describing what it means that God's Word is living and active, the EBC says simply, "It does things." Ha! But seriously, we intuitively know what that means. It just does!

But there's another way the Bible is different than any other book. When we read the Bible, we give the Holy Spirit fertile ground in which to work. In John 14, Jesus was talking to His disciples about the role the Spirit would play in their lives. In verse 26, Jesus said, *"But the Counselor, the Holy Spirit, whom the Father will send in my name, will teach you all things and will remind you of everything I have said to you."* When we engage with God's Word, when we, in the words of the psalmist, "hide it in our hearts," we provide the Spirit with material to work with. (Not to limit the Spirit's ability, but it's easier to be reminded of that which you've already encountered.) What an amazing promise!

When we read the Bible, we give the Holy Spirit fertile ground in which to work.

But what do these two points have to do with helping you cultivate a hunger for reading the Bible?

As you seek God through reading the Bible, even if it's difficult at times, and even if you approach it with a less-than-perfect attitude, the Word of God begins to work in your heart. **It searches. It convicts. It encourages. It fuels.** And since you were made by God to know Him, the Word has a quickening effect on your soul.

Couple this with the power of the Spirit working in you to keep God's Word in your mind and in your heart, and you quickly begin to see that just by encountering God's Word, you are drawn to re-encounter it.

It's a cycle. And through this cycle you are drawn closer and closer to God. The more you read God's Word, the more you want to read it.

Feed Your Heart, Not Just Your Head

This is very important advice. First, though, hear me say this: You need to "feed your head" to be an effective teacher of the Bible. You need to know information, understand context, and have an in-depth grasp of both the big picture of Scripture and unique issues. I know this can be an intimidating prospect, but it's just the way it is.

However, learning the Bible with teaching in mind isn't the only way to interact with it. In fact, we can actually work against ourselves if this is the only way we ever approach Scripture. Remember, if we're going to help students realize how awesome God and His ways are, we have to believe it ourselves. "Feeding your heart" is another way of engaging with the Bible.

What does it look like? Well, it looks a lot of different ways. It might look differently for you than it does for me. But here are some strategies for feeding the heart that have really helped me, and others, over the years.

Names of God

One of the most awe-inspiring ways to encounter God through the Bible is to engage with the different names Scripture ascribes to God, Jesus, and the Holy Spirit. Encountering the names the Hebrew authors used to refer to God is to encounter the many different sides of God: *Adonai-Jehovah* (the Lord our Sovereign), *Jehovah-Jireh* (the Lord our Provider), *Jehovah-Shammah* (the Lord is Present). . . . Each name draws out an aspect of God's character that in turn draws us nearer to Him. Knowing Jesus as "the Lamb of God" or the Spirit as the "Counselor" is to really know God!

You can find lists of these names online or in the concordance or appendices of many Bibles. What would it be like to spend a week or a month reading and meditating on these names and the accompanying Scripture passages where they're found? My hunch is that it might strengthen your desire for God.

Attributes of God

The idea here is really the same as the names of God, just with a different angle. One of the ways I personally engage with God through the Bible is by focusing on His attributes, or His defining characteristics. I know God is good because the Bible tells me so: "Praise the LORD. Give thanks to the LORD, for he is good; his love endures forever" (Ps. 106:1). I know God is forgiving because the Bible tells me so: "If we confess our sins, he is faithful and just and will forgive us our sins and purify us from all unrighteousness" (1 John 1:9). I know God is just because, you guessed it, the Bible tells me so: "He is the Rock, his works are perfect, and all his ways are just. A faithful God who does no wrong, upright and just is he" (Deut. 32:4). You get the picture.

Again, lists of God's attributes abound. Find them, then get to know God's essential nature through engaging with Him through His Word.

Praying through the psalms

Biblical scholars tell us that the vast majority of the psalms were used by the first Christ-followers in corporate worship. And of course, they are still used that way today. But for me, the psalms give an amazing voice to my relationship with God. When I find myself lacking that emotional, heart-driven engagement with God, I turn to the psalms and use them as prayers to God.

Take, for instance, Psalm 100. One way to read this is to mine it for cultural context, looking at the original language, and so on. I call this engaging with your head. It's a vital part of learning and following God's Word. But, engaging with our hearts is vitally important as well. So, what does it feel like to personalize the psalm as a dialogue with God?

What if instead of reading Psalm 100:3 silently, to yourself, like this,

> *Know that the LORD is God. It is he who made us, and we are his; we are his people, the sheep of his pasture.*

You personalized it and voiced it as a prayer, like this:

> *Lord, I know that YOU are God. I believe it in my heart. You made me, and I am yours! Help me delight in this today. Keep this promise in front of me. I am the sheep of your pasture, God. And you are my shepherd. Thank you for being this for me.*

To some of you this might feel a little weird, a little out there, and that's fine. I get it. But, I hope you can see in this small example the powerful difference this makes in engaging personally with God through His Word. The Bible was never intended to be dry, safe, and emotionless. It was meant to inspire us, to change us, and to motivate us to both seek God and to seek the expansion of His Kingdom on this earth. Praying through the psalms is a powerful way to see Scripture in this light.

Regular Means Regular

We defined this first best practice as "regularly seeking to know God through engaging with Him through His Word." Unfortunately for you and me—the super-busy, discipline-challenged, twenty-first century Christ-followers that we are—this is where we often find the biggest hurdle. The "regularly" in the definition gets us every time. As much as it presents us with a difficult bar, we have to be people who embrace the challenge.

Here's the deal: Do you have to carve out 30-45 minutes of every morning to do a "quiet time"? *No. You don't.* Is this a really awesome practice? *Yes.* Is it modeled by Jesus in the Gospels? *Actually, yes.* But we're interested in improving. And to improve, you might have to take baby steps, building up to the discipline of a daily, fairly time-intensive, and meaningful time alone with God. But there are other, if not better, ways to stay close to God through His Word.

There are a million means available to the modern Christ-follower to regularly encounter God through His Word. There are apps galore. There are phenomenal Study Bibles with all the content available on your phone, tablet, or computer. There are free podcasts of audio Bibles, and there are truly excellent, high-end audio Bibles. There are more study plans online than you could read through in a lifetime. You know the nice thing about all of these? They're mobile.

With all of the tools available to you, there's no reason that you can't spend some time each day—whether you're riding in your car or waiting for your child's practice to be over with—meeting God in the Bible.

A LITTLE TOUGH LOVE

I want to close this chapter with a little tough love. I don't want to put a guilt trip on you. I don't want this to feel like another sermon or lecture on why you should be doing your daily quiet time. What I want is to leave you with a challenge.

I want to start over with how you think about studying the Bible.

Somewhere along the way, you've lost your wonder.

You've lost your sense of fascination and awe with God.

As your life has grown more complex and the demands of each day more intense, you have begun to think of your time with God as a chore. A ritual. And you've begun to simply go through the motions. Or, more realistically, you've stopped doing it.

Stop for a second and think about a time in your life when you soaked up God's Word. Think about a time when you sought Him regularly with a real passion! When you felt close to Him.

OK, I meant it. Don't keep reading. Actually stop for a second and think about this.

Can you identify one or two factors that contributed to you having such a hunger for God?

Write them down on a piece of paper, a napkin, your arm, your friend's arm . . . wherever. Just visualize them. Think about them for a second.

Now, write down what changed. What's different in your life now?

I have a hunch that there's nothing most of you will write that's an insurmountable obstacle. My gut feeling is that with a pretty minor change in behavior you could put yourself back into that place. But, there's a problem. (Here's the tough love part I was telling you about.)

The problem is this: If you aren't making time to meaningfully engage with God through Bible study, knowing God in this way must not be important enough to you. It's not something you value.

What's keeping you from valuing the process of knowing God more?

What we value dictates our behavior. Do you go to the gym regularly? It's because you value your health, your appearance, or both. Do you invest your money? If so, it's because you value the idea of some level of financial security. Do you keep up your yard? Do you keep up your appearance? Do you spend time with your kids? Do you spend time watching TV? Whatever you do, you do it because you value it. Because it means something to you. And in the vast majority of cases, you don't do things because they're simply not important to you.

If you aren't regularly communing with God through interacting with Him in His Word, it's because it's not something you value.

So, I leave this chapter with a question: What's keeping you from valuing the process of knowing God more? Asked in a way that stings a little more: Why isn't it more important to you to know God better? Why can't you get up 30 minutes earlier five days a week to spend time in prayer and Bible study? (Trust me, I ask myself this question at times as well.)

The answer is that you can make it happen. But it has to be important to you. You have to value knowing God.

My prayer for you, and I mean this, is that you would do the soul work it takes to find that spark once again. I want you to want to know God more and better. I want you to hunger for His Word. I want you to have a thirst for a life that is influenced, informed, and impacted by your encounters with God through your engagement with His Word.

I hate to break this to you, but your effectiveness at teaching students the Bible is directly proportional to your own hunger for God and for His Word.

You'll never be the teacher you could be if you're not personally and regularly seeking God. If knowing God and living out of this knowledge is not important to you, it will show in your teaching.

I don't know you, but I'm betting the last thing you want to do is to communicate to students that it's not important to know God.

The first and maybe the best "best practice" is engaging with God. Without this, the rest of the practices are hollow advice.

Now that the foundation is laid, let's start building.

BEST PRACTICE #2:

Prepare WELL, TEACH WELL

The best preparation for good work tomorrow is to do good work today.—**Elbert Hubbard**

Preach the word; be prepared in season and out of season . . .
- 2 Timothy 4:2

What do the following stories have in common?

The Hoover Dam is a seriously impressive work of engineering. It's over 700 feet high and over 1,200 feet long. It required over 3.2 million cubic yards of concrete to build. Of course, a structure like this doesn't spring up overnight. The plans for the dam were over 100 pages long, and were completed years before the construction began! Planners created a city in the desert to house the workers and the engineering headquarters. The job was so big, it took thousands of workers over three years to complete it.[1]

In game six of the 2011 World Series, the St. Louis Cardinals beat the Texas Rangers to force a seventh and deciding game. In what many baseball experts have called the greatest game ever played, the Cards avoided elimination by coming back from deficits in the ninth and tenth innings. The hero of the game was David Freese, who tied the game in the ninth and won it in the tenth. But how he even got the chance to play in the game is a story in itself. Freese spent six years and 1,600 at-bats in the minors, playing for four different minor league teams with two different organizations. When he finally made it to the majors in 2011, his hot start was cooled thanks to an injury that cost him 51 games. But he stuck with it and came through when it mattered most.

On August 12, 2010, 10,267 Chinese men and women broke the Guinness Book's record for the longest human domino chain. The group, made up mostly of high school students (not surprisingly), took almost an hour and a half from start to finish to break the record. But getting ready took longer than that. To prepare, the students practiced four and a half hours a day for three days prior to the event. All the hard work apparently paid off for one young student named Li Xiaodong, who was the first person to fall. "While lying there, I thought about a lot of things," Li said. "But what I felt most strongly was the pure excitement that came from knowing I was part of the creation of a world record."[2]

So, what do these three stories have in common?

[1]http://en.wikipedia.org/wiki/Hoover_Dam. Accessed February 10, 2012.
[2]content.usatoday.com/communities/ondeadline/post/2010/08/10000-chinese-students-form-worlds-longest-human-domino-chain/1. Accessed February 10, 2012.

That's right. They all speak to the importance of preparation. The Hoover Dam wouldn't have been built if the massive preparation work hadn't been done. David Freese wouldn't have solidified his name in the lore of our national pastime if he hadn't put in his work in the minors, preparing for the biggest stage of his career. And our good friend Li Xiaodong wouldn't have gotten to feel the life-changing rush of world record breaking exhilaration if the team hadn't spent hours practicing how to fall backward. It's true. Preparation is key.

**WHICH LEADS TO OUR SECOND BEST PRACTICE.
BEST PRACTICE #2 IS THIS:**

To teach the Bible well, we must prepare well.

You want to be a great teacher of the Bible. I know this because you're still reading this book. You want to create powerful moments where students encounter God in ways that are real and transformative. And to do this, you have to be willing to put in the work to prepare. And to prepare well.

This is the moment where I pull back the curtain and let you in on a secret: **There aren't a lot of teachers who love to prepare.** It's true. If you don't like it, don't beat yourself up. The rush of the classroom is powerful. But preparing can sometimes suck the life out of you. You're not alone if you feel this way. But, I'm about to pass along a message that should give you hope!

The thing about preparation is that it doesn't have to be long or boring.

The thing about preparation is that it doesn't have to be long or boring. When done right, you can prepare to teach an awesome 30-minute Bible study lesson in just a few hours. Promise. And you can have fun doing it. We're going to spend a few minutes over the next few pages learning how to prepare well. But first, let's evaluate how you're currently preparing.

(NOTE: This chapter is the most involved, by far, of the *7 Best Practices*. But it's important, and hopefully full of the right kind of information to help you teach the Bible better. I do think, however, that this is a good time for me to explain something about this book. You don't have to read it from start to finish. If you feel like you have a good process, by all means, skim this section [looking for stuff that jumps out at you], but feel free to move to the next best practice.)

HOW DO YOU PREPARE?

Process is important. Believe me. It's less about the routine (study in the same place, at the same time, and so on) and more about the steps you're actually taking to prepare. Before I put my two cents in, I want you to take 90 seconds and think about your process. Think about what you do each week to prepare to teach. And I want you to think in terms of steps. So, start with Step 1, and go until you've completed describing how you prepare.

Describe your process start to finish below if you're reading these words on actual paper. If you're on an e-reader, again, jot your steps down on a slip of paper or in your journal. (If you don't fill in all the steps, don't worry. And if you need to add more, well, you're a stud.)

Step 1:

Step 2:

Step 3:

Step 4:

Step 5:

OK, so you've articulated your process. Be honest: Was this difficult? Did you have trouble writing down your process because you don't really have a consistent one? It's OK to admit it. That's why you're reading this book. For some of you, this may have very well been the first time you've thought about your preparation in these terms. If so, no worries. For others, especially you process junkies out there, you could list out your process in your sleep! Either way, the important thing to ask yourself now is whether or not your process serves you.

Think about your process, and think about how it translates into your teaching. Are there parts that you could pare away, time you spend that really doesn't serve you that well? Or did you find your process to be lacking? Do you have the feeling that you need a little more structure and intentionality to your preparation? If so, you've come to the right place.

A BETTER WAY

Let's look at what I believe are the essential parts of preparing to teach the Bible. I'm going to walk you through a sort of general process for preparation. As I go, think about the parts of this process that you didn't see on yours, or think about aspects you have that I may have left out.

Preparation Step 1: Pray

OK, so it's pretty basic. But basic doesn't mean trite or trivial. I make sure I enter every sermon, lesson, or even devotion preparation with prayer. I want to make sure I am in line with what God wants to do through me.

Why do we pray? A few reasons:

- Prayer is foundational! When we incorporate prayer as a part of our preparation, we align ourselves with God's agenda.
- God may have a message for your students in your class. Seriously. God may want to lead you in a different direction than your lesson may be taking, or than you had originally prepared for. There have been times where I was led in a different direction than I had planned or was given a fresh thought or a new direction because of time spent in prayer.
- Prayer opens us up to the Spirit's leading and what He desires to accomplish in our students.
- Prayer helps us realize that for the lesson to be effective, it needs to be about the Lord and not about us.

Can you prepare to teach God's Word without praying? Yup. But I try not to!

Preparation Step 2: Know Your Curriculum

There are three types of people reading this book: those who prepare all their lessons from scratch, those who use some form of curriculum, and those who do a little of both. This section is for those who use curriculum in some form. (Again, if this isn't for you, skip this section. I won't tell.)

It's important that you know your curriculum. What do I mean by that? Let me explain by starting with a big secret from a guy who's been developing curriculum for 10 years:

The best curriculum is nothing but a stepping-stone to a good lesson.

Like buying a suit off the rack in a department store, for it to work, it must be tailored. The same is true for your curriculum. Why is this the case?

The simple answer is that you know your students better than the men or women who wrote the particular lesson you're using. To be effective, you'll need to tailor each lesson to your group. We'll get into this more in-depth in a minute. But it is enough to know that part of your preparation is looking over your lesson from a big-picture perspective and identifying what you will keep and what you will need to adapt.

Here are some good questions to ask of your curriculum:

- Is there enough information to allow you to teach solid Bible Study?
- Are there any games or creative introduction types of activities?
- If so, do they work for your group?
- If not, do you want to create any?
- Is there enough interaction?
- Is it culturally relevant? Or do you need to think about some connection points for students?
- Is there an intentional focus on application?
- Are there denominational/theological considerations you need to address?

Once you've evaluated your lesson and seen where you need to do any additional work, you're ready to start getting to know the passage you're going to teach.

Preparation Step 3: Dig In

This is the point in your preparation where you get to know the passage you're studying. This is the fact-gathering moment where you're beginning to examine the passage from all angles. (Even if my curriculum provides me with some Bible commentary, I usually want to know more than the commentary that comes with lessons. I bet you do, too.) My digging-in process has five parts. Yours might be shorter or longer. But let's take a quick look at my model so we can have a baseline.

What does this look like for me? The first step is to simply read the passage. I read a passage several times, at least three to five times right out of the gate. The first couple of times I'm reading it to get a feel for it. It's unlocking the memories, thoughts, and lessons I've associated with that passage from times where I may have studied it before. There's not a lot I'm doing here, just trying it on for size. I make sure to read the passage aloud a couple of times as well. I'm not smart enough to know why this changes it for me, but it does.

At this point, I'll clear my head a bit, and get ready to slow things down. Now I'm ready to read it with a little bit of intention. I'll read the passage again, this time looking for clues to how I might teach the text. Here's a little checklist I go over in my head:

- I'm asking questions of the passage.
  - I'm not answering them yet, merely writing questions in the margins or in my journal. "What did Jesus mean when He said bridegroom?" "What did Peter mean by a holy priesthood?"

- I'm looking at any specific words that might be intriguing to me.
  - I'm circling them. I'm underlining them. Words that look important. Words that have concepts that might hinge on them.

- I'm looking for particular themes.
    - o I'm trying to identify any larger themes I might want to explore and find supporting Scripture for. If the passage is about forgiveness, I'm making mental notes of either other passages about forgiveness that come to mind or a word/theme search to do later on.

- And I'm writing all of this down with the goal of seeking the answers to these questions once I'm done.

LET'S TRY THIS TOGETHER . . .

Let's look at this following passage in 2 Corinthians 5:16-20. I want you to take a minute or so and work through the process I just dictated above. I've given you some space below it to record your thoughts. If you're reading this on an e-reader, I'd encourage you to grab a napkin or your journal and work through this process. Let's give it a go . . .

> [16]So from now on we regard no one from a worldly point of view. Though we once regarded Christ in this way, we do so no longer. [17]Therefore, if anyone is in Christ, he is a new creation; the old has gone, the new has come! [18]All this is from God, who reconciled us to himself through Christ and gave us the ministry of reconciliation: [19]that God was reconciling the world to himself in Christ, not counting men's sins against them. And he has committed to us the message of reconciliation. [20]We are therefore Christ's ambassadors, as though God were making his appeal through us. We implore you on Christ's behalf: Be reconciled to God. (2 Cor. 5:16-20)

Step 1: Read it a few times.

Step 2: Ask questions of the passage. Write them below or on a sheet of paper.

____

____

____

Step 3: Circle any intriguing/potentially important words in the passage. If you need to make notes about them for later, give it a shot below.

____

____

____

Step 4: Write down any particular themes this passage speaks to.

____

____

____

____

____

____

How was that process? Have you done anything similar before? Maybe this is something you're completely familiar with. Or maybe it's something you do internally. For some of you, this will be the first time you've done an exercise like this. Let me walk you through a super short list of some of my observations just to see if we're tracking.

Step 1: Read it a few times.

- (Done!)

Step 2: Ask questions of the passage.

- (v. 16) "Worldly point of view. . . ." What does this mean exactly? Probably need to define this.
- (v. 16) "Regarded Christ this way"? It was Paul who was speaking here, so that makes sense.
- (v. 17) What does it mean, biblically, to be "in Christ"?
- (v. 18) What does it mean that we've been given a "ministry of reconciliation"? Is this a different call than we see Christ give in places? Or is it the same? Hmmm . . .
- (v. 20) What does it mean practically that we are "Christ's ambassadors"?

Step 3: Identify intriguing/potentially important words in the passage.

- (v. 17) New creation?

- (vv. 18, 19) Reconciliation.
- (v. 20) Wonder if the Greek word for *ambassador* has the same connotation as our current understanding of ambassador?

Step 4: Identify key themes this passage speaks to.

- (v. 17) Where else does the Bible talk about being a new creation? Or this old life versus new life?
- (vv. 18, 19) Reconciliation is a big theme here. Might need to find other verses where this is supported or explained.

Step 5: The final step is to go find the answers!

Now, maybe these are answered really nicely in your curriculum, if you have the luxury of using a curriculum. But maybe they're not. And if not, you have to get the answers somewhere. This is where a great commentary, study Bible, or Bible dictionary comes in really handy.

I'm about to recommend some of the resources I've used throughout the years. This is not an exhaustive list, nor am I receiving any sort of compensation for recommending them. Furthermore, there's the chance that one of these resources may one day drop off my list, and others may jump on it. But as of my writing this book, these are some of the resources I've found to be essential to answering the questions I ask of biblical texts.

Study Bibles

A good Study Bible is almost an essential. My personal favorite is *The ESV Study Bible*, though I have found a lot of use out of the *NIV Study Bible* and the *Life Application Study Bible NIV*. Regardless of what you use, they are extremely helpful.

Commentary

Commentaries can be costly. But, I've found it to be economically doable to buy them one volume at a time, purchasing used copies on Amazon.com®, or by looking for sets on sale on eBay® and at clearance sites such as Christianbook.com®. My go-to commentaries over the years have been:

- The Expositor's Bible Commentary series
- New International Bible Commentary

- Some of the commentaries from InterVarsity Press
- Word Biblical Commentary series
- Weirsbe Bible Commentary series (love, love, love this resource)

Ask some of your staff members what they would recommend. And don't forget to allow for theological and denominational differences.

[Note: If you can afford to purchase any of the popular brands of electronic Bible Study software, there really is no better resource tool. But they're expensive! And many of them are geared toward academics or preachers, so there are a lot of tools that the average layperson would never use. But, again, they are incredible.]

Miscellaneous

There are a few miscellaneous resources that are vital to my preparation. First, a good Bible dictionary is always handy. (I prefer the *Holman Bible Dictionary* but there are a ton of good ones.) So is a Bible handbook. (*Halley's Bible Handbook* is my personal fave.) You'll be surprised how often you'll turn to these resources when it comes to answering specific questions. Two resources that are absolutely vital in my preparation are *Mounce's Complete Expository Dictionary of Old and New Testament Words*. Don't let the title fool you. This is one of the most intuitive and least intimidating language resources in print. It is awesome and perfect for lay people like you and me. Also, *Nave's Topical Bible* is a great resource to source your theme studies with. It organizes the Bible by topic, which is a really nice tool to have.

Preparation Step 4: Organize, Organize, Organize

So now that you've taken the time to ask your questions and used all your resources to answer your questions, what do you do? It's time to organize your thoughts.

If you're a curriculum user, this is where you'll have to kind of blend what the curriculum has given you with what you want to tweak, pull, add, and cut. But whether you build on an existing lesson, or if you're like me and basically start each lesson from scratch, how you organize your information is key.

I have a general outline that works for me. Yours may look different, or you may just go with the way the lesson is originally organized. My *general* outline for teaching always looks a bit like this:

- Introduction—This is where any icebreakers or thematic introductions happen.
- Passage Introduction—This is placing the focal Scripture passage in the context of its entire book, and the book in the context of the overall story of the Bible.
- Passage Study—I'll usually break this down into two subsections: original cultural context and the main theological truth of the passage.
- Application—This is the takeaway, how the main truth affects our life.

I have this outline in mind as I prepare and as I look at a curriculum lesson for the first time. I know when I start that I'm usually going to organize around this outline. Yours may be slightly different. What's important is that you have a plan.

Preparation Step 5: Practice

This one is simple, if often neglected. It isn't rocket science. And it isn't new information. You know that you'll be a better teacher if you simply go over your talk a few times. Make sure you're familiar with it. The more familiar you are with your lesson, the better you'll be able to allow conversations to go longer, or to follow other threads, and so on.

OK, so, this is the process that has served me and others pretty well over the years. What do you think? Look back over your list you made earlier.

What did I have that you didn't have?

What did you have that I didn't?

Hopefully, you were able to glean a new tip or two from what I've tossed out. But, I think it's important to know that there's not some magic formula. There's no right way to do it. What's important is that your preparation leads to dynamic classroom teaching. If that's happening, you're doing something right!

NOW WHAT?

Before we transition into our next best practice, I think it's important to make a point here about preparation that will help launch us into the rest of our best practices. When it comes to preparing to teach, the key is to know more than you teach. Always. Let me put this another way: Don't feel like you have to "get out" all the information you've "put in."

We need to be careful with how we relay what we've gathered in our preparation. Some teachers have the tendency to want to teach all the knowledge they've gathered during the course of their preparation. I've seen the effects of this type of teaching on the faces of beleaguered teenagers inundated with facts, points, and takeaways. It's not a pretty sight. We have to resist this tendency at all costs.

In her book *The Youth Worker's Guide to Creative Bible Study*[3], Karen Dockrey refers to how we "steal Bible Study learning" from our students. Karen wrote that we do this when we spend the week preparing and then basically dump a week's worth of preparation on them. In this scenario, all we're doing is simply regurgitating (my word, not Karen's) what we've learned. In most cases, students learn very little from this style of teaching. It's OK not to communicate all you've gathered in your preparation. Not only is it OK, it's probably for the best!

This line of reasoning is actually a good transition into the rest of this book. Most of the rest of the best practices have to do with the actual teaching of a lesson. My goal is to help you take what you've learned in preparation and lead you to be a dynamic, effective, and transformative teacher.

So, without further ado, let's move to Best Practice # 3.

[3] Dockrey, Karen. *The Youth Worker's Guide to Creative Bible Study.* Nashville: B&H Books, 1999.

BEST PRACTICE #3:
CONTEXT IS KEY

All Scripture is the context in which any Scripture is to be considered and applied.—**Anonymous**

And beginning with Moses and all the Prophets, he explained to them what was said in all the Scriptures concerning himself.
— Luke 24:27

EVERETT: It didn't look like a one-horse town, but try getting a decent hair jelly.

DELMAR: Gopher, Everett?

EVERETT: And no transmission belt for two weeks, neither.

PETE: Huh? They dam that river on the 21st. Today's the 17th!

EVERETT: Don't I know it.

PETE: We got but four days to get to that treasure! After that, it'll be at the bottom of a lake! We ain't gonna make it walkin'.

DELMAR: Gopher, Everett?

EVERETT: Well, you're right there. But the ol' tactician's already got a plan. [Everett fishes a gold watch from his pocket and tosses it to Pete.] For the transportation, that is. I don't know how I'm gonna keep my coiffure in order.

PETE: How's this a plan? How're we gonna get a car?

EVERETT: Sell that. I figured it could only have painful associations for Wash. [Pete pops the front and reads the inscription.]

PETE: To Washington Bartholomew Hogwallop. From his loving Cora. Ay-More Fie-dellis.

EVERETT: It was in his bureau.

DELMAR: You got light fingers, Everett. Gopher?

PETE: You mis'able little sneak thief! You stole from my kin!

EVERETT: Who was fixing to betray us!

PETE: You didn't know that at the time!

EVERETT: So I borrowed it 'til I did know!

PETE: That don't make no sense!

EVERETT: Pete, it's a fool looks for logic in the chambers of the human heart.

So, what's going through your head right now? A little confused? Unsettled? Trying to figure out what the heck is going on? If so, you have a good idea of how a lot of students feel in our Bible study lessons! Let me explain . . .

How this previous piece of dialogue affected you will depend on your level of engagement with movies. If you have no idea what you just read or where it came from, you probably struggled a bit to make sense of it. If you're a person of good taste who likes movies, you might have recognized this as a piece of dialogue from the excellent movie *O Brother, Where Art Thou?*[1] If you are a true connoisseur of fine cinema, you would know who played the characters, where this scene fell in the overall plot, and what the finer points of the dialogue were referring to.

But keep in mind, this movie is, at the writing of this book, nearly 12 years old. Even if you had seen the movie years ago, you might not recall the details. And if you've never seen it, this scene means nothing to you! Without context, you won't be able to grasp what's going on.

Watch what happens when some context is given. Imagine reading this paragraph first, then reading the dialogue:

> O Brother, Where Art Thou? *is a clever, artistic, and hilarious movie directed by the incomparable Coen Brothers. Starring George Clooney as Everett, John Turturro as Pete, and Tim Blake Nelson as Delmar, the movie is loosely based on Homer's The Odyssey. With Everett in the lead, the three main characters escape from prison and race against time to recover a "treasure" from Everett's dilapidated home before the government dams a river, effectively flooding the property. Set in the quirky and impoverished Deep South, the three cons encounter a host of eccentric and absurd characters along the way. One of these characters is Pete's cousin Washington Hogwallop, who, following the death of his wife, Cora, lives alone with his son on a run-down, dusty farm. Faced with putting up Everett and the gang for a*

[1]O Brother, Where Art Thou? DVD. Directed by Joel and Ethan Coen. Touchstone Pictures, 2001.

few nights or turning them in for reward money, Hogwallop chooses the latter, forcing the three men to flee the farm. But not before Everett collects a souvenir for his trouble.

See what a difference context makes? When given the big-picture plot and the events immediately following the scene, your understanding of the dialogue is dramatically improved. We can and should apply the same principles as we lead students to study the Bible.

WHICH SEGUES QUITE NICELY INTO A BRIEF DISCUSSION OF BEST PRACTICE #3, WHICH IS:

> Teaching in context is vital to students having a big picture understanding of the Bible.

This is the shortest chapter in this book, but one that may be the closest to my heart. I believe contextual teaching is one of the easiest, yet most powerful things we can do as we teach the Bible. Why do I feel so strongly about it? Easy: I want students to grasp the overarching biblical narrative. I want them to know the Bible story! I want them to know how the big pieces fall: how God moved powerfully and mightily across the ages to create all things, to create humans and call a people to Himself, and to constantly seek their redemption, most perfectly seen in the life, death, and resurrection of His Son, Jesus.

When we don't teach the Bible in context, Scripture loses much of its effectiveness.

When we don't teach the Bible in context, Scripture loses much of its effectiveness. The Bible becomes this loose collection of unrelated stories and isolated verses. Narratives become fairytales. Verses become isolated moralistic statements, not much different than an ancient proverb or the fortune in a fortune cookie.

Contextual teaching preserves the thread of the Bible's purpose.

Let's put some teeth to this best practice, shall we?

WHY CONTEXT IS KING

Do you tell a good story? Or know someone who does? Think of how you tell a good story. If you want to make the story have maximum impact, you set the stage. You take the time to provide the context for what you're about to tell. If you don't, you tell a story that's not nearly as meaningful because the listener doesn't know exactly how to place the story in a specific context.

The same goes with a good joke. If you rush to the punch line without building up the context, it falls flat. The surrounding context of your joke is what gives the punch line its punch.

The same is *especially* true of your Bible teaching.

Teaching any passage without providing the context is not only a poor way to teach, it actually does your teenagers harm. It fails to help them see the "big picture view" of Scripture. The fear is that instead of helping teenagers understand the Bible as the story of God's redemption of humankind, teenagers will see it instead as a mob of unrelated stories and moralistic teachings.

THE "HOW" OF TEACHING IN CONTEXT

So, how can you teach in context? Glad you asked. Here are three easy tips.

Think Macro

Before you teach any verse or passage of Scripture, take a few seconds to place the book of the Bible that verse is in into the overall timeline of Scripture. It can look as simple as something like this:

> "OK, today we'll be looking at a passage from Philippians. If we're thinking about where Philippians falls in the Bible, it's a New Testament book. It was written after Jesus died. The Church had started to spread after Jesus' death and resurrection. Philippians was written to a specific group of these new Christ-followers."

See? All you have to do is place the book in context with the rest of Scripture. It's vital for your students to know that Philippians isn't in the Old Testament. Paul wasn't a contemporary of Job. He was writing after Jesus had ministered and been crucified. This kind of "spatial understanding" of where a book of the Bible falls is critical to helping your students understand how the narrative of Scripture works. Do this enough with the different lessons you teach, and you will (almost inadvertently) help your students grasp the flow of the Bible's story!

Who? When? Why?

Go a step further and help your students grasp the particulars of a book as you teach it. Do this by answering three simple questions:

- Who wrote the book?
- When was it written?
- Why was it written? (In other words, what's its purpose?)

This stuff isn't boring. It's vital. And your students need to hear it. Do you need to treat them to a discourse on the alternate theories of the authorship of Genesis? Probably not. But students need to know that Scripture was written by God-inspired people, in a certain cultural context, with a specific purpose in mind. Take our Philippians example, and this looks something like this:

> *The Apostle Paul wrote Philippians. We all know Paul, right? Remember, Paul was the guy who had that amazing life change. He was the number one enemy of the church in Jerusalem. But, if you recall, he encountered Christ in that bright light on the way to Damascus. Jesus transformed Paul's life and mission. Paul became the biggest influence for Christianity outside of Christ Himself! Paul was writing to the Philippians somewhere around AD 62, or roughly 30 or so years after Jesus was crucified and arose from the dead. Paul wrote to the Philippians from prison in Rome. The reason for the letter was probably to simply encourage the Philippians to stay strong in their faith, and to thank them for their care and concern for him.*

With those two paragraphs, paragraphs that would take about two minutes, tops, to read, and might require all of about 5 minutes of research, you have given your students an awesome contextual foundation to build their understanding of Scripture on. It really is that simple!

Think Micro

Once you've set the stage for the book, don't just jump into a passage. Help students know where the passage fits into the surrounding text. If you're teaching your students Jesus' words from Matthew 7 about not judging others, place the passage in the context of the Sermon on the Mount. Take a quick second to summarize what was going on. The easiest way to do this is to simply go back a chapter or two and figure out exactly what was going on in the narrative.

FINAL THOUGHTS

Does teaching contextually take more preparation? Honestly, it does. But nothing a good study Bible can't solve! (Can you tell I love study Bibles?) Does it add three to five more minutes to your teaching time? You bet. But if your goal is transformation in the lives of your students, it's worth it.

You see, transformation doesn't happen without the Spirit speaking through the Word. And I believe contextual teaching provides your students with a much clearer understanding of the Bible. Clearer understanding leads to better application. And better application is at the heart of life change.

So, give contextual teaching a try. I promise you and your students will love it.

On to Best Practice 4!

"Gopher, Everett?"

(I couldn't resist . . .)

BEST PRACTICE #4:
EMBRACE
UNPREDICTABILITY

The fundamental qualification for teaching is learning.
—**Andrew McNab**

Now when he saw the crowds, he went up on a mountainside and sat down. His disciples came to him, and he began to teach them . . .
— Matthew 5:1-2

Many of you are familiar with TED. TED stands for Technology, Entertainment, and Design. TED is probably more recognizable to you as that wonderful collection of really, really awesome presentations by amazing people from all over the world[1]. (If you haven't discovered TED Talks, you're missing it. They are one of the best things about the Internet.)

One of my favorite TED speeches is from one of my favorite authors, Malcolm Gladwell. Gladwell is an eccentric and genius best-selling author and speaker. Gladwell was invited to speak to an audience under the pretext of talking about a concept from one of his books. But he instead shared the remarkable story of a psychophysicist named Howard Moskowitz. This fascinating anecdote is a really good introduction for our next best practice.

Moskowitz is semi-famous in the food service industry. When the synthetic sweetener aspartame was first developed, Pepsi™ went to Moskowitz and asked if he would do the research to find the perfect blend of aspartame to make the perfect Diet Pepsi™. Moskowitz did the research and discovered that, much to his surprise, there was no perfect Pepsi, only perfect Pepsis.

You see Moskowitz had meticulously engineered these focus groups to determine what percentage of aspartame garnered the most favorable reactions from people. But the research pointed out that there was no magic formula. People's tastes were too varied.

The significance of this, Gladwell related, was lost on Pepsi and on many other industry leaders. That is until Vlasic® came to Moskowitz asking for his help in creating the perfect pickle. Moskowitz replied with the zeal of an evangelist, "There is no perfect pickle, only perfect pickles." He urged Vlasic not to focus their efforts on perfecting their traditional pickle, but to introduce some variety, some choice, in the form of the zesty pickle. They did, and they were wildly successful.

The heart of Gladwell's story came when he told of Campbell's® asking Moskowitz to figure out the perfect spaghetti sauce for their struggling Prego® line. Of course, Gladwell says, Moskowitz answers with the line, "There is no perfect spaghetti sauce, only

[1] http://www.ted.com/pages/about

perfect spaghetti sauces." Moskowitz led a spaghetti sauce revolution. He propelled Prego to the top of the industry (and would later work for Ragu®, as well) because he realized there were multiple kinds of spaghetti sauce that people liked. There was not a perfect one; there were perfect ones.

And as Gladwell told it, this line of thinking from Howard Moskowitz is the reason there are multiple flavors of chips, crackers, vinegar, and soft drinks . . . and 36 varieties of Ragu spaghetti sauce!

There is no best way to teach a Bible study lesson. There is no perfect way. But there are different ways.

Gladwell sums up the great impact Moskowitz has had on our cultural relationship with food by telling a story about mustard and the search for the next, best mustard. Of course, by now we know what Moskowitz said. And it's what he said about mustard that will introduce our next best practice. Regarding the search for the best or perfect mustard, Gladwell relayed Moskowitz' words in this way:

> *"There is no good mustard or bad mustard. There is no perfect mustard or imperfect mustard. There are only different kinds of mustards that suit different kinds of people."*[2]

We can talk about the right mindset and the right way to prepare to teach teenagers the Bible. We can talk about the importance of teaching the Bible in context. But we have to remember one thing: There is no best way to teach a Bible study lesson. There is no perfect way. But there are different ways. And we need to embrace different ways of teaching. Why? Because our groups are made up of individuals with different personalities, different likes, and different makeups. We need to teach different kinds of Bible study lessons for different kinds of teenagers!

OR TO PUT IT ANOTHER WAY, HERE'S BEST PRACTICE #4:

> **To teach the Bible in a dynamic and transformative way, we must embrace unpredictability in our teaching methods and styles.**

[2] http://dotsub.com/view/100f2c6c-b178-4728-b653-f90cde33b522/viewTranscript/eng ; http://www.ted.com/talks/malcolm_gladwell_on_spaghetti_sauce.html Both accessed February 14, 2012.

When was the last time you radically changed the way you taught your class? For some of you, teaching in a variety of different ways just comes naturally to you. But for others, you've taught the same way for years and years and years. Week in and week out, your lessons are as predictable as the rising sun. Even if you are a great communicator, you'd be surprised how much more effective you'd be if you switched it up every once in a while. This concept is at the heart of this chapter.

In this chapter, we'll examine some of the philosophy behind why we should vary our teaching methods, and how to go about doing it. We'll look at a ton of sample activities so you can get some ideas, and finally we'll close with a look at how Jesus modeled this best practice Himself.

THE NEW THINKING ON LEARNING STYLES

It used to be, years ago, that I would jump in to a discussion on learning styles. In many ways, it's been the sort of go-to for talking about variety in teaching. We're still going to use this concept to guide us, but I would be remiss if I didn't mention a new development related to this concept.

If any of you were education majors in college, or have had any sort of teaching training in the past, you've no doubt looked at the concept of learning styles. The traditional take on learning styles is that people are more or less hardwired to learn in certain ways. Though there are several different theories that identify different categories of learning styles, one of the more traditional ways of thinking about this concept is by looking at these three categories:

- Visual learning
- Auditory learning
- Kinesthetic or tactile learning

The three categories are mostly self-explanatory. Traditional wisdom says that if you're a visual learner—you guessed it, seeing is learning! The visual learner grasps concepts easier through charts or images, and might visualize images in her head while she's learning a concept. Auditory learners are people who, according to the theory, are more inclined to learn by hearing. The auditory learner may process knowledge while humming, or may need to read aloud to better retain information. Finally, the kinesthetic or tactile learner needs to associate learning with activity. The kinesthetic learner would need to build or do something with his hands for the concepts to really take root.

This sacrosanct principle of educational theory has one caveat: Learning styles don't seem to be nearly as hardwired as they were thought to be for the last half century.[3] It's not that people don't have preferences to learn in certain ways. It's simply that people are able to learn through a variety of different methods and experiences. Not only that, researchers also found that by switching up how knowledge is delivered, actual knowledge retention may be increased. (So much for the whole "study in the same place every time" theory.)

I took this little side road into academia with a purpose in mind. I want us to do two things based on the findings of this and similar research: I want us hold on to the whole learning style concept, though with a different focus, and I want us to be teachers who embrace the idea of variety when it comes to our teaching.

Furthermore, I think it's important to talk about learning styles because of a truth I've observed over the years: If we're not intentional about changing things up, we'll inevitably default to *our* preferred method of learning/teaching. That may not always be a bad thing. But, it will definitely be our preferred method, which may very well not be the preferred learning method for some, most, or any of our students! That's why intentionality is key. We have to intentionally change things up. Learning styles are a great way to help us think in terms of new teaching methods.

Don't think of learning styles as rigid gateways we have to account for with our students or else they won't learn the Bible. Think of them as ways to help us come up with different *teaching* styles. Even though learning styles may not be as hardwired as we once thought,

[3] http://psi.sagepub.com/content/9/3/105.abstract Accessed February 14, 2012.

there's still good reason to believe that many people simply have a preferred way they like to learn. We can use learning styles as a starting point in varying our teaching styles. Embracing the traditional learning style concepts enables us to teach God's Word with a lot of variety.

USING LEARNING STYLES TO STEER TEACHING STYLES

If our goal is to provide variety in the classroom, then we can look at learning styles as a catalyst for finding different teaching styles. Let's go down each learning style and list some teaching activities under each. This way, you'll have a good variety of activities you can practically implement in your teaching. Once you get in the habit, it becomes almost second nature to think about adjusting your teaching to account for these different learning styles.

If our goal is to provide variety in the classroom, then we can look at learning styles as a catalyst for finding different teaching styles.

Visual Teaching Styles

To appeal to students who seem to prefer visual learning, we need to think in visual terms. Regardless of whether you're using an existing curriculum or writing your own lessons, you can adapt or tweak any lesson to include some visual learning elements.

Recall that those who prefer visual learning like to at least see or associate images with what they're learning; this image association may actually help them retain information. These students may benefit from your facial expressions or body language. And you may even notice someone who's visually inclined, closing his or her eyes to picture a concept or story.

So, some suggestions for visual learning activities could be:

- Showing a video to introduce a lesson.
- Drawing diagrams or pictures on a dry erase board while you teach.

- Using your placement on a stage or in a room strategically. (In other words, when you make an important point come to the front of the stage, or otherwise incorporate your positioning.)
- Setting up an "image walk" on the walls of your meeting space, with images that relate to the theme of what you're teaching, for students to look at and somehow respond to.
- Making an outline on a dry erase board as you teach.
- Showing a clip from a TV show.
- Doing an object lesson where you bring in an object that somehow connects to what you're teaching.
- Having students act out a skit. This can be recorded ahead of time and edited by one of your students.
- Using presentation software to show images that accompany your teaching.
- Using props of any kind to illustrate your lesson.
- Having students paint or draw as you teach or as a way of introducing a lesson.
- Pulling pictures of modern-day Biblical settings from the Internet and showing them on a projector or printing them to distribute.
- Using different colors of markers to make different points on a dry erase board.
- Coming up with some sort of a humorous tie-in between your lesson and a piece of clothing, and then wearing that clothing while you teach.
- Changing the decorations in your room every once in a while.
- Using light or darkness strategically in your teaching.

Auditory Learners

Auditory learners learn primarily through listening, through the actual act of hearing the information being taught. But it doesn't stop there. Many people who prefer auditory learning activities also find that discussions and conversations help them retain knowledge better. Lectures suit the audible learner quite well. Audible learners are the ones who are dialed in to what you're saying most of the time.

What are some examples of auditory learning activities? Here are just a few:

- Storytelling or reading aloud a narrative from the news or pop culture.
- Exploring different sounds. (For example, I've taught a lesson on Pentecost several times over the years where I download voices reading the Bible in different languages, then couple it with the sounds of wind. I play them as I read the Acts 2 passage. It's amazing how the story comes alive, especially for those students who prefer to learn audibly.)
- Reading the Bible aloud for these students makes a difference.
- Bringing in podcasts that somehow relate to the passage or topic you're teaching.
- Listening to audio Bibles.
- Accessing public domain audio files. You can download famous speeches and other interesting historical audio from the National Archives[4]. It's a fun way to bring in history as context.
- Interactive lectures where there's a lot of discussion.
- Debates work wonders for audible learners. Have two teams, and assign them either side of an argument or issue. Instruct them to formulate their argument then present it.
- Music! Of course music rules for audible learners. Find music that has a thematic tie in to what you're studying.
- Asking students what sounds may come to mind when they read a certain passage of Scripture.

Kinesthetic Learners

Those teenagers who prefer to learn in the kinesthetic or tactile model learn through doing stuff! They need to be moving around, active, tossing a ball or other object, or even playing with a pen or marker. People who identify as kinesthetic learners might learn better by simply getting up and moving around during the lesson. In fact, many of your kinesthetic learners tend to go nuts when they've

[4]http://www.archives.gov/

been in one place for too long! The find it challenging to sit still for long periods of time, and are easily distracted if they aren't up and moving.

So, last but not least, what are some teaching styles that might work for these kinesthetic learners?

- Facilitating a hands-on learning activity such as sculpting, finger painting, or building.
- Role plays are awesome! What if you had students act out the parts of a biblical narrative?
- Providing students with an object to hold on to that has some sort of tie-in with your lesson.
- Creating an art walk where they draw or construct images that represent some key truth or concept as they go.
- Blowing up balloons or constructing a model as part of an activity.
- Stations are simple to facilitate and they work wonders for kinesthetic learners! Have different learning stations where a narrative or a passage is laid out in several stages in your classroom. Or ask multiple choice questions and have students go to lettered corners based on their answers.
- Something as simple as having students stand if they believe the answer to a question is yes or sit if they think it is no.
- Relay races or obstacle courses are great ideas, though hard to do outside of an introductory activity.

Hopefully you realize that there's a nearly limitless amount of options for you to implement in your efforts to embrace unpredictability. The idea of this section is simply to get you thinking about how you can change things up in order to more effectively engage your students, and to create some unique experiences that may serve as anchors to the biblical knowledge they're learning.

VARIETY IN YOUR ENVIRONMENT

Bringing variety to your teaching doesn't begin and end with the actual activities you choose to incorporate. You can create a ton of unpredictability by varying your classroom set up. And as far as this goes, your creativity is the only major inhibitor. (While having a big budget makes room set up easy, with a little creativity you can pull off a really cool experiential environment for very little money.) Let's think about some general ways you can embrace unpredictability in your teaching environment.

Set Up

You'd be surprised how new and fresh things would feel if you'd simply rearrange your chairs from time to time. And again, new research shows that this novel change in environments might actually help students retain your Bible teaching better. Have fun with this. Go from rows to a big circle one week. Then, after a few weeks, switch to chairs seated around multiple tables. Or, get rid of the chairs altogether. Have students sit on the floor, or find as many throw pillows as you can and scatter them around your room. However you do it, simply changing your room set up can have a big impact on how unpredictable your teaching feels.

You'd be surprised how new and fresh things would feel if you'd simply rearrange your chairs from time to time.

Thematic

Don't be afraid to get crazy and really embrace your lesson's theme. If you're studying poverty, recreate a slum in your classroom. Bring boxes of trash in and strew it on the floor. Build huts out of cardboard. Teach sitting down while students stand around or sit on the ground. Daniel and the lion's den? Recreate a lion's den by making cardboard cutouts of lions, and use brown, crumpled wrapping paper for rocks. (I had a friend who, for his lesson on the Lord's Supper, recreated a first century Jewish meal, complete with a low table and pillows and carpets laid out around the table.) Doing a lesson on being light in a dark world? Completely black out the room and teach by candlelight. The sky is the limit! Have fun, embrace your creative side, and do some really cool room set up around your lesson's theme.

WHAT ABOUT TECHNOLOGY?

In many ways, we're still learning how the massive amount of data teenagers take in on a daily basis is affecting their ability to learn and comprehend. Certainly technology is playing a huge role in this ongoing discussion. Technology delivers tremendous stimulus and information at the tap of a screen. Researchers seem to just be on the front end of figuring out how this onslaught of information influences the way students learn and the way we teach.

In light of this, how should you see technology as part of the best practice of keeping your teaching unpredictable? First, in the vast majority of suggestions I made in the previous sections on learning and teaching styles, technology can and probably will influence the variety you bring into a classroom. It goes without saying that as people who work with teenagers, we're pretty much surrounded by advancing technology. Hopefully by now you've come to embrace at least some aspects of it in your classroom settings.

Second, as I alluded to earlier, technology is having an effect on how students learn. As we seek to stay in touch with learning theories and research, we have to know how to involve technology in our ministries so that it functions as a learning tool, not some sort of marketing tool, and certainly not mere entertainment.

We need to search for ways to teach the timeless truths of Scripture by using methods in line with how teenagers are becoming more and more conditioned to learn. You can rarely do this by standing in front of a room and lecturing from a written lesson plan. If you care about your students knowing God and living out His ways, you'll be committed to looking for ways to stay fresh in your teaching. Much of this revolves around embracing technology in your ministry context.

JESUS EMBRACED MULTIPLE TEACHING STYLES

As people deeply interested in helping teenagers encounter God through the Bible, we have an awesome model in Christ Himself.

Jesus went to such great lengths to embrace a variety of teaching approaches. Don't believe me? Look for yourself . . .

- Jesus embraced lecture. Think about the Sermon on the Mount in Matthew chapters 5-7. We don't see Him doing a whole lot more here than just teaching.
- Jesus made time to simply chat people up. This is informal teaching at its finest. Think about His conversation with the Samaritan woman at the well. Life-changing? You bet. Formal? Anything but.
- Jesus embraced interaction. In so many cases, He engaged people in discussion. The Pharisees, the sick, His disciples, Nicodemus, even Pilate. He was constantly interacting as He taught truth.
- Jesus asked awesome questions, and He did so with a direction in mind. He led people to where He wanted them to be and then let them discover truth for themselves.
- Maybe more than anything, Jesus used a ton of examples His audience could relate to. He was the ultimate culturally relevant teacher! He sprinkled His teaching with metaphors and analogies using sheep, seeds, vines, trees, birds, and so on. He helped make connections that people could immediately understand.
- Jesus focused on practical application of principles! He said, "You have heard that it was said, 'Do not commit adultery.' But I tell you that anyone who looks at a woman lustfully has already committed adultery with her in his heart" (Matt. 5:27-28). He said, "Go and do likewise" (Luke 10:37). Over and over Jesus said, "Do not worry," "Do not be afraid," and "Do not do as they do." Jesus was very interested in seeing people's lives practically affected by the gospel.
- Jesus was all about creative and often kinesthetic teaching! He rubbed dirt with spit and put it in people's eyes! (Ha! Try doing that with your students!) He drew on the ground with a stick. He used object lessons. (Fig trees and mustard seeds anyone?) He multiplied bread and fish. He pulled coins out of a fish's mouth.

Jesus understood what we must also understand, that people are inclined to process and learn differently. He embraced it and His teaching shows it. We must strive to do the same.

FINAL THOUGHTS

Paulo Freire, the educational theorist, had a theory he called the "banking" concept of education. In this concept, the student is viewed as an empty account to be filled by the teacher. Friere's theory set up the analogy of students as merely receiving objects, receptacles into which we as teachers deposit knowledge. I'm pretty sure I speak for you when I say this isn't what we want from our Bible study time! Your desire to see your Bible study time come alive and be deeply meaningful to students is why you're still reading this book! So let's review one last time the importance of embracing unpredictability.

The goal is transformation. Ultimately that's the Spirit's role. But anything we can do to help is icing on the cake!

To recap, if we're not intentionally embracing unpredictability in our teaching by focusing on various teaching styles and activities, we'll inevitably default to our preferred learning style. The problem is, of course, that this neglects the preferred learning personalities of our students. The importance of keeping things varied is so we might reach all of our students in ways that they most comfortably relate to.

The goal is transformation. Ultimately that's the Spirit's role. But anything we can do to help is icing on the cake!

Now, on to Best Practice #5!

BEST PRACTICE #5: PLAN FOR INTERACTION

It is not what we learn in conversation that enriches us. It is the elation that comes of swift contact with tingling currents of thought.—**Agnes Repplier**

As iron sharpens iron,
so one man sharpens
another.
- Proverbs 27:17

I delivered much of the content in this book in a workshop at *Group* and *Simply Youth Ministry's* 2011 Simply Youth Ministry Conference. One of the reasons I love this conference so much is because of the great level of training that takes place on a smaller scale throughout the week. This workshop was no different. It was full of some great folks who shared a lot of awesome content. No doubt, some of their input made its way into these pages. I was inspired by the passion of the youth workers I encountered, and I continue be inspired.

One of the more lively exchanges took place as we talked about the importance of planned interaction. I had planned a little activity in which I asked a volunteer to lecture us about a banana. The purpose was to demonstrate how much more learning and how much more fun happens when there's interaction as opposed to straight lecture.

I began by calling a volunteer to the front and handed her a banana to use as a reference. She turned out to be pretty spunky, and what ensued was a really fun interaction that will probably not translate fully to this text. But it demonstrates my point well.

I set the stage by explaining that the volunteer would be pitching this banana concept to us, a hungry group of men and women. The only thing is that we have no solid concept of what a banana is. We've never really encountered a banana other than maybe hearing about one, or maybe seeing one in passing.

I asked this young lady to communicate to the group the ins and outs of a banana, what the benefits were, why a banana was desirable for satisfying hunger, what a banana tasted like, and so on. But there was one catch: No one was able to ask questions. She could only explain based on her ideas and concepts of what a banana was.

Here's a transcript of how the interaction went:

ME: [Handing the volunteer the banana, stepping to the side.]

VOLUNTEER: [Looking at the banana.] OK, well. . . . Um, for the women, if you have cramps, a banana will totally kill them . . .

CROWD: [Laughter.]

ME: [Interrupting, slightly uncomfortable.] Wow . . . I never knew that . . .

CROWD: [More laughter.]

ME: And I love that you lead with that, by the way . . . [Shaking head.]

VOLUNTEER and CROWD: [Laughter.]

VOLUNTEER: It also, in the morning, uh, in the morning if you need a pick-me-up, it's got great energy. If you're like, "Oh, snap, I have to leave in five minutes!" *Bam!* In the car, on the way to work, you can pop it open and eat it, but please leave one hand on the steering wheel!

CROWD: [Laughter.]

ME: Just my luck, I choose a banana expert as a volunteer.

VOLUNTEER and CROWD: [More laughter.]

VOLUNTEER: Um . . . [Long pause, searching.] It's easy to open.

At this point, I stopped the volunteer who was actually doing a pretty entertaining job, but had started to slow down a bit. I told the crowd they were free to ask questions about the banana from the perspective of people who had seen bananas before, but had not really ever experienced one.

Watch what happened when I allowed the audience to ask questions . . .

QUESTION 1: What did you mean when you said, "pop it open"?

VOLUNTEER: [Realizing she had not demonstrated how to open it.] Oh! You take the stem of it and . . . [Demonstrates opening the banana.]

QUESTION 2: Can you eat the peeling?

VOLUNTEER: No!

QUESTION 3: What's inside?

VOLUNTEER: It's squishy?

QUESTION 4: How's it taste?

VOLUNTEER: It's got a firm but squishy taste; it's kind of a fruit.

The questions go on like this for another minute or so. And they're coming rapidly. People got clever and funny with their questions, and we had a good time with it. By the end of this short exercise, a great deal of interaction had taken place, and a great bit of knowledge about bananas had been shared!

Here's the point. At the beginning of this volunteer's spiel, she did a great job, but it was one-sided. There was no engagement. And the focus of her entire talk was based on her understanding of the banana. She communicated what she felt was important about the banana, based on her experiences. *I mean, good for cramps?* What an off-the-wall first comment! But a humorous one that demonstrated my point perfectly. When we lecture, it's always about us even if we don't realize it. But open up the discussion and it becomes about us all!

When the discussion opened up, people began to ask about taste, function, and characteristics. And the volunteer was spurred on to take paths she did not take on her own. This is such an awesome example of why interaction is key. And it brings us to our fifth best practice.

BEST PRACTICE #5 IS A POWERFUL ONE . . .

> To lead students beyond a surface-level relationship with God and His Ways, we must strategically plan for interaction.

Here's the deal: Organic conversation happens all the time during the course of teaching the Bible to teenagers. Some of it's beneficial; some of it's a distraction. But interaction that leads to real life change doesn't usually happen by accident. And truth be told, if we aren't intentional about it, interaction may not happen at all.

I've found this to be true in my own teaching over the years: When I don't prepare, I'm more prone to lecturing. You may be the opposite. But I find that when I'm most prepared, I account for moments of interaction in my teaching. Call it interaction with a purpose.

Let's take just a little time and talk about the "whys" and the "hows" of planning for meaningful interaction with your students.

WHY IS INTERACTION IMPORTANT?

Look, I'm no learning theorist, and by this point in the book, that's pretty evident, right? I could talk about upper level cognitive functions, but I would only be borrowing other people's ideas, and I'd probably do it in a way that made simple stuff complex. So, I'll save us all the trouble with the complex academic explanations. I look at it this way . . .

We can preach at or lecture to teenagers, and we can do an awesome job at it. We can love God, we can prepare like crazy, and we can teach in context. We can do all of these things and still miss the mark in a big way. We're concerned with teaching Truth. And I don't know about you, but I want to teach it in a way that cuts through the noise of a teenager's world. I want to teach the Bible in a way that says to our students, "This is important. Let's stop and talk about this." I want them wrestling with their thoughts. I want to provide opportunities for them to agree or disagree with me. I want them to own their thoughts and beliefs.

When I don't prepare, I'm more prone to lecturing.

None of these things ever happen in a one-sided lecture. Ever.

If you think about it, so much of what passes for learning in a teenager's world is simply knowledge intake. This isn't a knock on teenagers. It's just true. They get information in bite-size chunks, a 140-character blurb here, a status update there. Whether it's a Tumblr© post, a billboard or magazine ad, or a text, teenagers are engaging with shorter and shorter bursts of data more frequently. And they aren't taking a ton of time to really process much of this data. Again, not good or bad. It's simply where we find ourselves as a culture.

I'm OK with it. I'll take technology any day of the week. But you know what? I also want to be the guy that says to my students, "Let me show you a better way. Let me put God's Word in front of you. And oh, by the way, I'm going to ask you to think about it. And to talk about what you're thinking about. And chances are after that, I'm going to push back a little on what you said in an effort to make you think some more." This level of engagement is the least we can offer our students!

If we want to see real life change in teenagers, we have to be strategic about creating scenarios where they're internalizing God's truths. This happens in real, dynamic discussions.

HOW DO WE PLAN FOR INTERACTION?

There's no mystery here. If you're using curriculum, the hope is that there's some space created in the course of your Bible Study time for a discussion. Now, as I've said earlier, all curricula are meant to be tweaked, even the curricula we produce. Based on your students, you'll almost always need to either beef up or tone down the questions. So, if you're using a curriculum, check over your questions, see which direction you need to go in, and use some of the following tips to address your time of interaction.

If you're not using curriculum, you'll need to carve out space to engage students in discussion. There's really no time that's bad for interaction. You can and should plan for it in some form or fashion in the beginning, middle, and end of your lesson. As you are thinking about how you'll craft a thematic introduction to your lesson, think about how you'll engage students in discussion. Do the same thing as you're crafting your Bible study time and as you're crafting the closing of your lesson. The tips below will help you think in terms of what this looks like. Blocking it out is the easy part.

(NOTE: I set the bar pretty high on curriculum. I'm picky. And one of my personal dislikes is lesson plans or discussion guides that have teachers teach long passages, or have them sermonizing for long periods of time, to be followed by a few questions. I think with learners of all ages, you'll lose many of them in these long blocks of lecturing. I try really hard to have a little burst of Scripture, then some interaction, then another burst of Scripture, then some interaction, and so on. It's a preference thing; there's certainly no right or wrong way to do it. But I find that I can keep the mood in the class pretty high and keep people engaged when I make room for multiple points of interaction.)

Crafting good questions isn't easy.

WHAT DOES THIS LOOK LIKE?

In the sections that follow, we'll examine some very practical ways to go about planning for interaction. But first, let's address sort of a foundational point—namely, the art of asking good questions.

Asking Good Questions

As someone who has designed Bible study curricula for almost a decade, I can say this with absolute authority: Crafting good questions isn't easy. While it comes easier for some than for others, it's still a skill. It's something you have to just get good at. Now, you've probably heard this before in some shape or form. But there's a reason why good Bible study questions are tricky.

When you talk with your friend over coffee, there are probably only a small percentage of questions that you really think about before you ask them. Most of the questions flow effortlessly out of the conversation. The nature of why you're together dictates the context, and with the exception of very serious or weighty conversations, most of the interaction just sort of happens. This ease of conversation is a byproduct of your friendship and of the relaxed feel of your gathering.

However, when we're leading teenagers in Bible study, the nature of your gathering is completely different than a chat over coffee. The context dictates an entirely different purpose for asking questions. But, with a little intentionality, you can ask great questions of your students, leading them to comprehend and apply what you're studying.

I kind of think about a movement or a process as my philosophy of asking good questions. I'm trying to start at one level and move students up the ladder of learning. How does this process look? Something like this: First of all, I ask questions that are knowledge based. For example:

How did Jesus meet the physical needs of the people gathered around Him and of the disciples?

For this question, there's a right answer. Second, I want to build on the knowledge they've uncovered and move them to deeper thinking. I want students to go beyond mere information and to begin to synthesize some of this knowledge. So I ask questions that challenge them to really look at the story from all sides, evaluate it, and come up with an answer that shows a level of deeper reflection. I might ask a question such as this:

Why do you think the disciples seemed to have a really good grasp of who Jesus was at some points, and yet seemed to completely miss the point at others?

Finally, all of my questions should be designed to lead somewhere. For students who are more mature in their faith, I might ask questions that lead to deeper questions. This would be my destination or my purpose in this case. But in most cases, I'm trying to lead students to a point where they begin to see how to apply the knowledge they've learned to their lives. So, this line of questioning might look like this:

What are some ways that you can show the world that your identity is found in Christ? What does that look like for a teenager in a twenty-first century context? How can you practically live this out in your daily life?

So that's a little glimpse of a thought process that leads to asking good questions. Here are two things you didn't see in my sample questions. Call them my pet peeves of question asking:

- Pet peeve 1: Yes/no questions
- Why: They rarely ever lead anywhere. Most times, they accomplish very little.
- Example: "Did Jesus ask Matthew to follow Him?" Ugh . . .

- Pet peeve 2: A million knowledge-based questions
- Why: An abundance of knowledge-based questions that don't lead to deeper thinking will wear students out. And anyone else who is listening.
- Example: "What did Jesus say to the disciples? What did Jesus do after He said that? What happened after they got to the other side of the lake? What happened after that?" See? I'm bored just typing that!

OK, so those are some types of questions that drive me nuts. In the interest of fair play, here are some questions I like. It's not an exhaustive list, but here are a few different categories of questions you might ask your students:

- **Knowledge-based questions**—We've covered this already, but you have to ask some knowledge-based questions to establish the basic facts of the story. The point is that you need to move on from there.
- **Questions that establish emotional context**—When used properly, these questions help set the stage for the emotional climate of the passage.
    - o Examples: What do you think Peter might have been feeling at this time? What clues are there in the text that this was a tense situation? How would you have felt if you were in this situation?
- **Compare and contrast questions**—Comparing or contrasting stories, verses, responses, and so on is a great way to get students thinking deeply about Scripture.
    - o Examples: What are the similarities between Joseph's and Daniel's situations? How are Peter's call to be holy and Paul's call to imitate Christ similar? Compare the thief's response to Christ with Pilate's. What similarities do you see? What differences?

- **Debate or evaluation questions**—These questions lead students to take a stand on an issue, or to form an opinion and then wrestle with it! This requires a deeper level of thought and learning, but is crucial to helping students own concepts.
    - o Example: Do you think Jesus meant that we have to forgive people even if they haven't shown any remorse for how they've wronged us? Explain your answer.
- **Application questions, part 1**—These questions try to help students take what knowledge they've learned and apply it in a unique or novel situation.
    - o Example: How does Jesus' role as mediator affect the way you seek God in prayer?
- **Application questions, part 2**—These questions lead students to consider what changes might result in their actions or attitudes from learning a specific concept.
    - o Example: What are three ways you can obey Jesus' command to be "salt and light" in your family context this week?

(BONUS: Here's a bonus from me to you. I'll let you in on a little bit of information passed along by someone who's been leading teenagers in spiritual development for years. In the July/August 2010 edition of Group® Magazine, youth ministry veteran Duffy Robbins passed along what he called "The 5 Arenas." Duffy described the five arenas in which a teenager does life as follows: school, family, social life, personal life, and church community. Here's the secret: I keep this list on my desk. When I write a Bible study lesson I will often refer to this list to make sure I'm asking questions that relate to all or several of these areas. I'd suggest the same thing to you.)

As I said, there are certainly more categories of questions than these, but these will help you get started in the right direction.

INTERACTION GRAB-BAG

Following is a loose assortment of guidelines that speak to planning for interaction.

Silence Is Your Friend

If you've been a teacher of any sort for more than about, oh, I don't know, four minutes, you know that the silence that comes after a question can be an unnerving experience. But, it doesn't have to be. Think about silence in a few ways. First, teenagers need time to process, especially if you're asking deep questions. And, there's actually a trick for taking the silence's sting away. Before you start your interaction, you could always say, "These questions are going to require you to flex your muscles a bit! If you need a few seconds of silence after each one to gather your thoughts, that's cool."

However, silence might mean you need to rephrase the question. I use the seven-second rule. I wait about five to seven seconds, no longer than seven, and then I'll rephrase the question. I'll wait another five to seven seconds and only then will I answer it myself. And a lot of times, I'll try one more time to coax an answer out. Don't let silence freak you out. It's just a part of teaching teenagers.

Discussions Are Journeys. Know Where You Want To Go.

You need to know where you're headed before you start a discussion. You are the guide. And though you can take a detour here or there, you need to have that GPS firing in the back of your mind. Know where you are at all times, and know where you're headed.

One way I've always done this is to think of a discussion in terms of a funnel. I've used this when writing group discussions that were to occupy a 30-minute time slot, and when writing three-question discussions. Think of the top of a funnel with its large opening. It's designed to catch whatever you're pouring into it. Think of your first few questions as just big, loose, catchalls. Top-funnel questions are 30,000-feet flybys designed to get you thinking about the general direction or theme of the discussion.

Mid-funnel questions tighten the focus. If your first question was, "Who likes sports?" your mid-funnel question might be "Who likes baseball?" (These are pretty crummy questions, but, hey, I'm over-simplifying to make a point.) The goal is to move toward the end of the funnel where you're laser-focused on whatever the main point of the lesson or line of questioning is. So, in our admittedly over-simplified thread of example questions, the bottom-funnel question might be "Do you like the Red Sox?" (See how I worked my fav baseball team in there? Nice, huh? My work here is done.)

Rabbit Chasing And Preparation

"Chasing rabbits," or following a line of questions that get you off course, can be a discussion killer. But here's a secret: The better you've prepared, the better protected you are against discussion-killing rabbit trails. If you have a solid idea of how the lesson plays out, and if you've really looked at all sides of a passage, you can be much more adept at allowing the discussion to veer here or there without really doing any damage to the goal you're gunning for. It's yet another positive side effect of doing diligent prep work.

The better you've prepared, the better protected you are against discussion-killing rabbit trails.

Listen On Your Toes

Don't use the time when students are responding to look at your notes. I've seen teachers do this, and I've done it myself. Hear me say this: Don't do it! Your job is to move the interaction along. Discussions are just like a fire. You have to tend to them or they burn out, no matter how hot they may start. When a student is answering you, you need to be actively listening. You need to be picking up on what he or she is saying, and what's not being said. You need to be listening, but you need to be thinking about a follow-up question. Remember, know where you're going!

Body Language Is Important

Use positive reinforcement and non-verbal cues to coax students to keep talking. Nod your head. Say, "Mm-hmm." If they're recounting something painful, show understanding in your facial expression. If what they're saying is funny, smile like a big, silly goofball! By all means, whatever you do, don't just sit there staring at them. Nothing squelches discussion like a facilitator who seems disengaged.

Reframing/Restating

If you want to drive me crazy, be the guy or gal who asks a question and then doesn't say anything when it's answered. Makes. Me. Crazy. The best facilitators of discussion are those people who can ask a question, listen well, and then either ask a follow-up question or summarize the response back to the person answering. This validates a teenager's response, increasing the likelihood that he or she will speak up again.

If you want to drive me crazy, be the guy or gal who asks a question and then doesn't say anything when it's answered.

Breaking Into Groups

Here's a super easy idea: If you have a larger group that seems to make discussion a little tricky, you can always break into smaller groups for break-out discussions. I've found that groups of no less than four work great for this way of facilitating interaction.

FINAL THOUGHTS

Planning for interaction takes a little work. Maybe that's what you're realizing about all of the best practices. But if a little more work ensures that our students are getting the depth they deserve from our teaching, isn't that extra work worth every minute? Again, I'm just the guy that says teenagers deserve better. God's Word deserves better.

We're getting close to landing this plane!

Let's keep moving . . . on to Best Practice #6.

BEST PRACTICE #6: TEACHING FOR APPLICATION

Biblical truth has been given to change lives, not simply to stimulate discussion.—**Dick Dowsett**

He replied, "Blessed rather are those who hear the word of God and obey it."
— Luke 11:28

I'll start this chapter off a little differently than previous ones. I want to relate a very short story to illustrate a point I'm going to make about this sixth best practice. Here's my story . . .

I have a friend who, because he changed careers in his early 30s, found himself in a season of pretty significant financial restraint. The problem is that he's a gadget-obsessed tech head. And we all know that a super geek with no budget is a sad super geek. This was around the time that the iPhone® 4 was releasing. If you recall, which you do if you're a Mac fanboy like me, the iPhone 4 was a pretty significant jump in user experience compared to the 3GS, and especially compared to the 3G.

Now, my friend had been an iPhone 2 early adopter years earlier. But his finances were such that he was unable to upgrade to the 3 or the 3G. Remember: super geek, tech-obsessed, gadget freak. To many this was no big deal. To my friend? The deal was most definitely big.

Long story short, I ran into my friend at a gathering. His eyes lit up.

"Hey," he said excitedly, "Check this out!" Out of his pocket he pulled an iPhone 4.

"Whoa," I said smiling. "Look at Mr. Big Shot! How in the world did you pull that off?" He began to tell me a story that bordered on ridiculous about how he seriously lucked into a brand new iPhone 4 that cost him a mere $50. Now, this was $50 he didn't have, per se. But some deals are too good to pass up. And, I have to admit I was genuinely happy for my friend.

"Congrats, man! That's huge," I said, patting him on the back. "Are you loving it? I mean, compared to your current piece of junk, this is like a Ferrari™! I bet you're pumped to be back in the world of the iPhone. How are you liking it?"

I could tell when I asked him that something was slightly amiss.

"Well," he said, kind of sheepishly, "It's not activated."

"Wait, huh? What does that mean?"

"I mean it's not turned on. It's not activated. I don't have the money yet for the data plan, so I'm just sitting on it until I do. But that's rad that I got one, right?"

I wanted to be happy for my friend, but all I could do was just stare. I was seriously speechless. I couldn't formulate a response. And then I just started laughing. I mean, really laughing. The image of my buddy holding a new iPhone that didn't work, carrying it around in his pocket (I mean, he had a case and everything), and showing it off to folks at this get-together was just too much. For whatever reason, it just hit me the right way. I could not stop laughing.

My buddy got all mad at me, for a second, and then I convinced him of how ridiculous the concept was. Like wolves on a fresh kill, a few of our other friends came over to see what I was laughing at. And of course, I threw him under the bus. Within a couple of seconds we were all having a pretty good time with it, even my buddy with the ~~brick~~ iPhone 4.

Here's a very simple truth: Scripture can't be taught absent of application. By its very nature, the gospel message compels the hearer to act!

The reason why this was so funny is because an iPhone, or any smartphone for that matter, isn't supposed to be separated from its ability to function properly. When robbed of a network and/or a data plan, the most expensive phone in the world is nothing but a piece of glass and plastic.

A phone with no network is a phone existing outside of its essential nature.

(Ready for the transition? Here she goes . . .)

In the same way, when we teach the Bible to teenagers separated from a focus on how the Bible changes our lives, we're separating the message of the Bible from one of its intended purposes.

Here's a very simple truth: Scripture can't be taught absent of application. By its very nature, the gospel message compels the hearer to act!

God's Word and His ways are designed to motivate change. Jesus surely modeled this in His teaching. In fact, His first public words of instruction, the first words we ever heard Him preach with authority, were dripping with application: "Repent, for the kingdom of heaven is near" (Matt. 4:17). James, Jesus' brother and the leader of the Jerusalem Church felt this way, as well. He gave us this wonderful summation in James 1:22: "Do not merely listen to the word, and so deceive yourselves. Do what it says." James said in verses 23 and 24 that hearing God's words and walking away unchanged is as logical as looking at yourself in a mirror, walking away, and then forgetting what you look like.

The Bible is remarkably clear on this: Belief was never separated from behavior. Life change was the expectation.

This life change is the heart of what it means to be a Christ-follower. We hear the gospel. We take in this information and internalize all that Christ did for us and all that means. And then sometime later, maybe moments, maybe decades, we believe what we have heard or read. And in that moment, this mysterious and wonderful Spirit-led exchange we call regeneration occurs. By it, and through it, we are saved! Salvation is ours.

Christ lived the life and did the work. We learn of the life and the work, and we believe it as Truth. And through this belief, we are set free. Reborn. Transformed.

We are *at once* sanctified, or made holy, through Christ's work on the cross, but we also begin a *process of sanctification!* (This concept never gets old! What an amazing thing! God is so cool . . .) The Spirit works in us to lead this process of sanctification to empower Christlikeness. But it's fueled by a growing knowledge of God . . . a knowledge that comes primarily from Scripture, and a knowledge that undergirds this life change.

This spiritual life change that occurs is most outwardly seen through the living out, or application, of God's ways.

AND BEST PRACTICE #6 IS ALL ABOUT APPLICATION:

> **To teach the Bible as it was intended to be taught, we must utilize it as a launching pad for life change.**

In short, we have to know how to teach for application. It is never enough to teach for knowledge. The wave that is God's mission has no room on it for information collectors. If we or the students we lead want to join God where He's at work in this world, it will happen because we're all radically applying the truths of God and His ways in our lives. Our goal in this chapter is to help you identify some very practical, very simple ways of beginning to embrace application in your teaching.

Let's follow the similar pattern we've followed thus far. Let's define what we mean by application, and then let's look at some sample activities of ways we might actually teach for application.

WHAT DO WE MEAN BY APPLICATION?

Information Applied To Students' Vision

This speaks to the idea that we can take new information, information about God and His ways, and apply it to how we see the world around us. It's a worldview-shaping kind of application. This happens when we encounter truths like Paul's words in Ephesians 2:8-9: "For it is by grace you have been saved, through faith—and this is not from yourselves, it is the gift of God—not by works, so that no one can boast." When we internalize truth on this level, the application that results isn't first a change in actions or attitude. (Though, those certainly flow from it.) This kind of application is vision affecting. It's an application of truth to our understanding of our lives. It's reorienting our belief structure around the central truth of God and His ways.

Information Applied To Students' Hearts

There's also a kind of application that affects what we value. This happens when we internalize a truth and it shapes what we see as important. One of the most obvious ways I've seen this over the years is when teenagers really understand God's Kingdom ethic of looking after the needs of those Matthew referred to as "the least of these." This is one of those earth-shaking shifts. Why? Because we're not inclined to take care of strangers, especially if it involves sacrificing our resources. But when a student reads a verse like James 1:27 ("Religion that God our Father accepts as pure and faultless is this: to look after orphans and widows in their distress and to keep oneself from being polluted by the world"), and they really get that God cares deeply about the poor and wants His children to as well, they begin to value this. The plight of the outcast and the impoverished becomes important to them.

This type of inward application is usually evidenced in a more outward action, such as sponsoring a child through *Compassion International* or through volunteering at a local food pantry. But the outward action is evidence of an inward change, a change in values as a result of encountering a knowledge of God's character and/or God's values.

Information Applied To Students' Practices

This is the type of application most of us think of when we begin to talk about life change, when a teenager's actions demonstrate an internalization of information. Let's say a student internalizes God's Kingdom value of loving your neighbor. The next day at school she refrains from gossiping about that girl who's always so catty toward her. Or, imagine a student really understands the Bible's teaching on sex that's acceptable to God. When this student refrains from going too far with his girlfriend as a result, this is application that's realized in practice, or behavior.

This type of inward application is usually evidenced in a more outward action

Now that we're on the same page, let's look at how you can actually incorporate this best practice in your teaching.

WHAT DOES TEACHING FOR APPLICATION LOOK LIKE?

There are a few ways we could go about doing this. I think the best way for us to push forward is to operate in much the same way we have throughout this entire book. Since this book is designed to be a resource that's driven by practical examples you can actually implement in your classroom, let's use the previous three types of application as our guide.

For each of the previous three types of application, I'll pass along a list of different activities you can do to facilitate or encourage the specific type of application. I want to say this before we move on:

As with any book, there will be some of these activities that you'll be inclined to try, and some you won't. There will be some you look at and say, "Oh, my students would love that!" and some you'll look at and say, "My students would never go for that." I get it. But I think these, and all activities suggested in this book and similar books, can serve you in a variety of ways.

Many of these truths take years to internalize. It's the nature of bending our sinful selves into a Christ-shaped person.

I'd advise you to try some of these out in your class, even some of them that might not suit your personality. But I'd also challenge you to look at them as starting points for generating your own ideas. Take the following activities and adapt them. Or use them as catalysts to come up with entirely new activities. They're simply meant to help you begin to think about how you can lead your students in application.

Application That Changes Students' Vision

If I'm being transparent, I'll confess that these first two types of application can be tricky to really hone in on in a single activity. Think about it: Can a five-minute activity really change students' view of life based on their knowledge of God? Of course not. Many of these truths take years to internalize. It's the nature of bending our sinful selves into a Christ-shaped person. But, we can begin to address this type of life change. In any individual lesson, our goal with this type of application is merely to get students thinking in the right direction.

So, without further ado, here are some activities that you can try to help students apply their knowledge about God and His ways to how they see their world:

- **Word clouds**—On a dry erase board, write the concept you're studying in one or two words, say "forgiveness," for example. Ask students to brainstorm categories or areas of their lives that forgiveness impacts (such as family, friends, relationships, and so on). Write these "areas" in their own circles away from the main word, but connected by lines. Then, for each of these areas, list all the ways forgiveness shows up in these categories.
    - o *Technology option*: Use an online mind mapping website and a projector to build your word cloud live. Do a Google™ search on it! There are tons of them.

- **Case studies**—This is a super old school approach, but in name only. Narrative and story are concepts that this generation of teenagers love. So, tell a short story where the main character is faced with some sort of ethical dilemma. Craft the story in such a way that it allows your students to apply the truths you've been studying to the situation. Have students respond with how the character should proceed in light of the biblical knowledge you've just covered.
  - *Technology option*: Have your students write and shoot a short film (or films). Arrange to show it in class.
- **Music**—Listen to some secular music that relates to, or more specifically, conflicts with the principle you've just learned. Have students voice exactly why the lyrics or message of the song conflicts with what you've learned. *(So, I know some of you are freaking out a bit. And I get it. The idea of playing secular music that obviously flies in the face of God's ways wouldn't cut it in your ministry context. Let me say to you that a) I understand, and b) we have to help students actually discern culture! We can't just tell them it's wrong. And c) obviously, there are lines that can't be crossed. I'm not saying bring in gangster rap. The average Selena Gomez song provides a double dose of worldly values in a relatively harmless package.]*
- **TV or movie clips**—Same exact activity as the music one, only with video instead of music.
- **Answer one question**—Give students index cards and something to write with. Ask one question related to the application of the concept you've been studying. Instruct students to answer in one sentence. Maybe you ask, "How do you encounter God in His creation?" Have students write their responses down without putting their names on their cards. Then, take them up and read them aloud. Or better yet, display them around the room.
- **Personal reflection activities**—There are quite a few ways to do this, but the idea is to lead students to sort of look inward and apply a concept to how they personally see things. This can be done in silent reflection with music playing. Or you can have students paint a word that represents an emotion brought up by the principle. Or you can give students an object, such as a pebble or a ring, to visualize this internal change.
- **Junk drawer**—Empty your junk drawer at home. (C'mon, I know you have one.) Supplement it with weird kitchen utensils or yard implements. Bring any other knickknacks you

can find. Dump them out where students can see them. Ask students to choose an object that represents some aspect of how the knowledge they've gained has changed or can change their lives.
   o *Technology option*: Have students take pictures of something that represents the principle you've addressed, or the change they need to make. Instruct them to make these pictures the home screen on their phone to remind them of the lesson during the week. Consider having them email or text them to you to post on your website or Facebook™ page.

Application That Changes Students' Hearts

Here are a few activities that you can use to help students apply their knowledge about God and His ways to begin to affect what they value:

- **Self-portrait**—Sum up the principle you're teaching in one statement such as, "Jesus wants us to tell others about the difference He's made in our lives." Then, have your students draw a self-portrait. When they've finished, have them personalize the statement (for example, "Jesus wants me to tell others about the difference He's made in my life,") and write it on their portraits.
   o *Technology option*: Same activity but instead of drawing pictures, students take pictures on their phones.
- **List building**—A great way to get students to begin thinking about how their values can change is to get them to write lists where they put things in order of priority. You can have them order the specific principle you've studied to see where it ranks in their lives.
   o *Technology option*: Do the same basic activity, but have students search for images that represent items on their lists instead of writing them out. They can share their images with the group, post them to a class Flickr® or Facebook page you're viewing, or Facebook message them to you or an assistant who's working a computer or projector.
- **What if?**—Have students describe what their lives would look like if they embraced the specific value. Have them be as descriptive as possible.
   o *Technology option*: Have students go to separate places in the room and record voice memos on their phones describing the same thing. Then, have them play back

the memos for the group when everyone is done. You'll be surprised how different this is when you're hearing recordings instead of your own voices. It's powerful.

- **Action plan**—This one is simple. Have students identify what changes would need to be made in their lives to actually reorder their values according to the principle you covered. Make sure they address specific challenges as well as specific opportunities.
- **Community action plan**—This is basically the same concept as the previous activity, but with a corporate slant. Ask students to consider what impact they could make if their community of friends collectively adopted this value.
- **Cultural narrative**—Find an example from popular culture of a person (ideally a teenager) who lived out the specific principle or value in a powerful way. Maybe this is a teenager who was persecuted for standing up for their faith, or a young adult who moved to Africa to start an orphanage. Read or allow a student to read the story and have a follow-up discussion to let students process.
    - *Technology option*: Find a story on a blog or a website where you can actually display it on a screen.
- **I will**—Distribute some sort of paper for students to draw on, maybe something like cardstock or cardboard. Make it fairly small, maybe the size of their hands. Have some markers and colored pencils available. Then, let students create a picture that represents the value you've discussed. Allow them to share how it represents this value in their minds. Then, have them write the words, "I will" over it. Have them keep this in a prominent place where it will remind them to begin to embrace this value.

Application That Changes Students' Practices

Finally, here are a few activities you can use to help students apply their knowledge about God and His ways to actually change their actions or practices:

- **Bad, good, best**—This can be super fun. Have two students role-play scenarios that allow them to demonstrate what the application of the specific concept would look like. So, if you're studying Jesus' call to be peacemakers, you could have three friends, two of whom are in an argument. Have students act out three scenarios: first the "bad" in which they do the opposite of what they should

do, then the "good" where they kind of do the right thing, then the "best" where they model a solid application of the concept. Discuss it afterward.
  - o *Technology option*: Video and edit the role-play, and then post it later in the week.
- **Three ways**—Simply list three ways they'll demonstrate living out the particular concept in their actions in the upcoming week. Your goal will be to help them actually narrow in on specific, doable actions.
  - o *Technology option*: Have students write their lists as a text. When they've read it aloud, have them send it to you. Text it back to them later in the week as a reminder.
- **Modeling**—Some practices can be modeled while you're meeting. If you're studying prayer, or Bible reading, or service, you have the chance to allow students to model it in your group environment.
- **I did this, now I do this**—On a dry erase board or a sheet of butcher paper, draw two (or more, depending on the class size) life-sized silhouettes. Think of the concept you studied. Is it a concept in which the application would primarily be head (thoughts), heart (will, emotions, identity, concern for others, and so on), or hands (a task or practice)? Identify which one of these the principle addresses. Then on, next to, and all around that specific area (head, heart, or hands), have students write on the first silhouette how they currently or used to think, feel, or act. Then, on the second silhouette, have them write how they think, feel, or act now as a result (or how they will in the future).
- **One way**—Simple. Have students identify one thing they'll do in the upcoming week to put this principle to work in their lives. When they've thought of their one way, have them say the sentence aloud, such as, "One way I'll live out [insert the principle here] in my life this week is by ____________________." Explain that you'll be texting them this week to check in on them, and you'll all be reporting back next week on how it went. *(Don't mess this up! Follow-through is huge! Don't forget!)*
  - o *Technology option:* Have students film a super-short video once they've actually completed their "one way." Compile them into one and upload to YouTube™, or have them post them on your group's Facebook page. Arrange to watch the videos in the next meeting.

- **Written on your hand**—This is basically the same concept as the last activity, but with a twist: Come up with a letter or two to that serve as a reminder for them of their "one way." Then, have them write those letters inconspicuously on their hand or their palm. Instruct them to go over the letters in pen or marker each day until they actually put the principle to work in their life.

Again, by no means are these exhaustive lists! They're merely ideas to get you thinking in the right direction.

Well, we're one stop away from the end of our journey. Let's move on and wrap this trip up!

Here comes the final best practice . . .

BEST PRACTICE #7:
KNOW YOUR
ROLE

"Anyone who breaks one of the least of these commandments and teaches others to do the same will be called least in the kingdom of heaven, but whoever practices and teaches these commands will be called great in the kingdom of heaven." — Matthew 5:19

And so we come to the final Best Practice. I hope this has been a meaningful experience for you. I've enjoyed the thought of some of you learning a great deal about becoming a more effective teacher of the Bible. Hopefully another group of you (who could have written this book yourselves) have gleaned a few tips here and there. That gets me pretty pumped up too.

My hope is that regardless of your experience level, you found something in this book that ultimately helps you lead students closer to God.

The purpose behind this final Best Practice is much less about technique or methodology, and more about inspiration. I want to spend part of these last few moments we have together leaving you with a bit of encouragement. We'll do this through examining the roles you play as someone who teaches the Bible to teenagers.

BEST PRACTICE # 7 IS AS FOLLOWS:

> **To be the most effective teacher of the Bible you can be, you must be aware of the many roles you play as you teach the Bible to teenagers.**

But before we jump into the roles you play as teacher, I want us to think about your students for a moment. Picture them. See their faces in your mind. (Even the ones who act like they don't listen to a word you're saying!) After all, this book really is mostly about your students and your opportunities to lead them closer to God. So, as you're thinking about your students, I want to ask you a question . . .

Who do you want to see them become? What do you want the result of the Bible coming alive in teenagers' lives to be?

What if you could, say, sit down with your students' parents and together shape a picture of what their children would look like when they graduate your church's ministry? What would that picture look like?

Now this is a pretty fun thought, isn't it? If you really begin to think about it, your mind can go in a lot of different directions. You could think in terms of character, or personality. You could think in terms of how students use their giftedness. You could think in terms of students pursuing their passions. And none of these would be wrong. But I want us to think in terms of what the Bible says about what the life of a real Christ-follower looks like. Specifically, I want us to look at what we can learn from looking at the lives of the disciples.

BIBLICAL CHARACTERISTICS OF A CHRIST-FOLLOWER

If we think about the disciples' lives, we realize there are some characteristics they embodied that we should desire to see lived out in our students' lives, as well. We might even go as far as saying that this is one way of thinking about the fruit of our time spent leading students to engage with God through the Bible.

The supernatural aspect of the Bible makes it different than learning anything else.

By no means is this a comprehensive list, but maybe just the ones that stand out the most to me. (I'm curious what characteristics you would add.) These different characteristics are as follows:

Learners

The 12 disciples were learners. They experienced the coolest seminary in the history of the world, a three-year degree taught in Jesus' classroom. Jesus constantly taught these guys principles of the Kingdom, then backed it up with practical application. The disciples were constantly in an environment of learning.

The supernatural aspect of the Bible makes it different than learning anything else. We know that most people don't read a chemistry textbook and beg for more. But the more your students know about God, the more they're compelled to want to know more. If you give your students a knowledge of the Bible and show them how to practically put it to use, they'll become learners who are hungry for more knowledge of God.

Teachers

The disciples were teachers. Think about it: Peter's sermon at Pentecost; Philip's encounter with the Ethiopian; and of course, James and John's commitment to teaching in their epistles, just to name a few. When your students take seriously the call to live out their faith, they teach their peers everyday what it looks like to follow Christ, mostly in their actions but in their words as well. The hope is that this example leads to relationships, which leads to an encounter with God through the Bible, which hopefully leads to a saving relationship with Christ.

The ways of God's Kingdom go directly against the ways of our culture in so many different aspects.

As you think about how you can incorporate some of what you've learned in this book, keep in mind the expectations you communicate in the course of teaching, or the lack of expectations, can actually shape how your students see their responsibilities to share what they've learned of God and His ways. If you expect your students to become people who teach others about God, your teaching "voice" and strategy will reflect this. If you lead them as those who will be leading others, you'll watch many of them actually become teachers.

Rebels

The New Testament picture of Christ-followers is one of a bold group of men and women who fully understood their identity in the face of a hostile world. These folks faced all kinds of discomfort because they rebelled from the values and expectations of their society. They chose to live by the Kingdom values taught to them by Christ. They were rebels.

Your students are called to be rebels, as well. The ways of God's Kingdom go directly against the ways of our culture in so many different aspects. If your students live as those who boldly resist the values of our society and who instead both radically pursue God's ways and infuse the world with the hope of the Gospel, not only will they be obedient to Christ's commands, they'll draw others to God. And as teachers, isn't that what we want?

Leaders

The disciples were leaders. Maybe more than anything, I want the students in my small group to become leaders too. I want them to lead those around them in how they think about their future and the values they attach to things like money and career. I want them to lead others in how people should be treated, especially the sick, the poor, and the cast-offs. I want my students to lead others in how to live out the ethics of God's Kingdom. And I want them to ultimately lead others to a true understanding of what a relationship with Christ looks like. I know you want the same thing!

I want my students to lead others in how to live out the ethics of God's Kingdom.

Keep these desires in mind as you prepare to teach and as you teach students the Bible.

Failures

The disciples were failures. Think about it: they failed over and over again. They said dumb things. They did dumb things. And they sometimes didn't do things that wouldn't have been dumb. Which is dumb in itself! But you know what? They failed because they were trying. They failed because they were giving it a shot. They were making it happen. And Jesus was cool with their failure. He took every single opportunity he could to use their failure to shape and mold them. He never once gave up on them.

If you aren't watching your students fail, chances are it's because they aren't trying. As much as you can, help your students understand that spiritual growth is a process. And as with many processes, there are moments where they may feel like they're taking a step backwards. Help them see that trying and failing is a huge part of learning.

KNOWING YOUR ROLE

Now that you've been challenged and hopefully encouraged to see your students in a different light, let's turn our spotlight toward you.

As we move to wrap this book up, I want to ask you to think about one final concept. If I asked you to consider what your role is as a

Bible study teacher, how would you answer? Take a moment and formulate a response if you want. Done? Cool. Because I have my own answer for you right here. And it's coming in the form of a challenge to you.

Consider this the post game talk after the big win. We've shared a good bit of time together, and we're about to part ways. Before we do, I want to send you out on a high note.

And so . . .

You Are Motivator

That's right. You are the cheerleader. You are the person with the microphone. One of your roles is to get students fired up about encountering God through the Bible. Why do teenagers need motivating, you might ask. Isn't the Bible awesome enough? Yes, it is. But we aren't. And even though their intentions were good, your students have heard the story of the Good Samaritan 20 times over the last few years by people who might not be the awesome Bible study teacher you are. But you're going to make the story of the Good Samaritan come alive for your students! Why? Because one of your roles is motivator, that's why.

You Are Inspirer

In one of my favorite episodes of *The Office*, Michael Scott (the deeply incompetent, but blissfully unaware boss of the Scranton office of Dunder-Mifflin Paper played by Steve Carell) is to give an inspirational talk at the local university's business school. Of course, he completely mucks it up in a way only Michael could. He tried to be inspiring, but he came across as insulting and lacking any real business knowledge. As he is attempting to come to grips with his performance later on in the episode, he and his protégé, the eccentric wacko, Dwight Schrute (played by Rain Wilson), have the following exchange:

Michael: What is the most inspiring thing I ever said to you?
Dwight: Don't be an idiot. Changed my life.

Now, most of your students will have a higher bar for inspiration than Dwight. (Even if they didn't you could probably still do better than "don't be an idiot.") However, I believe that each of you have just as great of a potential to inspire as Michael did.

I believe you can be someone your students remember the rest of their lives. I mean that. Do you know how you can accomplish this? Challenge them. Expect a lot from them. Tell them that the God they are encountering in the Bible desires for them to live powerful lives of purpose on mission for Him. Help them see that their lives are the single most valuable investment they have. If they aren't giving their lives to God to be used at His pleasure and for His glory, they're failing to make the most out of the gift He's given them.

Teach your students God and His ways and inspire them to follow Him accordingly.

You Are Master Storyteller

Something hit me about ten years ago. I realized how amazing the story of the Bible is, and how powerful the stories in the Bible really are. I came to Christ as a young adult. And so, many of the Bible stories I had gleaned as a child seemed like maybe that's all they were: children's stories. Then I learned them as an adult. I still haven't lost my love for just how BIG the stories in Scripture are.

Don't sell the Bible short! Tell the stories of Scripture as they are intended to be told! Not as boring, irrelevant, sterilized anecdotes, but as real, dramatic, life changing vignettes from God's amazing and ongoing story to redeem all of humankind. You can do this! Give Scripture its due. Make the sounds, sights, setting, and emotions of the Bible stories you teach become real for your teenagers. Pour yourself into being a master storyteller of God's Word.

You Are Ringleader

Put simply, you have to keep the show going. Sometimes it's hard. OK, a lot of times it's hard. But hopefully you're teaching because somewhere in you, you felt God's call to do so. Let that call motivate you to be the person who makes sure the action doesn't stop, the content never dries up, the stage is set as it should be, and there is always excitement for more. It can be a thankless job . . . from an earthly perspective. But the eternal investment you are making by teaching teenagers the Bible is not lost on God.

Don't give up. Don't give in. You're the ringleader. Own the ring.

You Are Prophet

Maybe you know this already, but the New Testament gift of prophecy speaks more to a "right telling" of God's Word than the ability to predict the future. The New Testament understanding of the gift of prophecy is more about being able to take the Word of God and powerfully, truthfully, and faithfully preach and teach it, cutting to the heart of those who hear it. In this way, you are a prophet to the students whom you teach. You have the ability to teach God's Word powerfully and directly. You can show students that the God of the Bible is no impersonal, irrelevant deity, but that He is alive and immediate! And that His Word, when heard and followed, can build us up to be purposeful agents of Kingdom change.

You can show students that the God of the Bible is no impersonal, irrelevant deity, but that He is alive and immediate!

Be a prophet for your students. Teach the Bible. And teach it well.

FINAL WORDS

And so, our time together has come to an end.

More than anything, I pray that the time you invested in this book has brought a return. I hope you can sense my passion for this subject, but also my humility. I certainly don't claim to know the only way, or even the best way. And I know if I could spend time with many of you, I would learn so much from your passion and experience. I simply pray that the words in this book have helped you in some way, large or small.

Finally, I am deeply thankful for you. I know we don't know each other, but I am so grateful for the sacrifice you make to lead students to encounter God through teaching the Bible.

You are my hero. And I truly mean it when I say it. Because of this, I want to genuinely extend the offer to help you if you ever need it. I won't put my contact info here, because, you know, email addresses and web sites change. But I promise you'll be able to find me with a little help from Google. If you need anything, shoot me an email. I'm always available to help out.

Keep the faith! When you get tired, keep going. You're not alone. The Spirit is empowering you to do the work He has called you to do. And that's a pretty cool thing!

God bless you and your ministry.

ACKNOWLEDGMENTS

First things first . . . There are two people who made this book come alive. In a lot of ways, Brandi Etheredge serves as Art Director for **ym360** (except when she graciously lets me play the role). Brandi took this book from a concept to the really nice piece you're holding in your hands. I'm thankful for her role on the **ym360** Team. She makes us look great. I'm also thankful for Lynn Groom, the most professional copy editor/copy writer I've ever worked with. Lynn is a magician. If this book is any good, it's because of Lynn. If it's not, it was probably somewhere I didn't take Lynn's advice. Lynn, thanks. I want to thank Dr. Allen Jackson for shaping so many of my thoughts about youth ministry, spiritual development, and life in general. Dr. J, you probably don't know what an impact you've had on my ministry. On behalf of thousands of guys just like me whom you have deeply impacted, thank you! Thanks to Scott Heath, Minister of Students at my home church. Scott, thanks for allowing me to lead students to encounter God through the Bible, and for putting up with my soap-box rants while we eat burritos. I'm thankful for Les Bradford, co-founder of **ym360**, who shoulders extra burdens when I work on a project like this. One of these days I'll actually stick to a production schedule. OK, maybe not . . . And finally, to my dear wife, Brendt: Thank you seems like such small words for the sacrifices you make so I can do what I do. There are good, supportive wives, and then there is you . . . an amazing, godly, selfless encourager who never falters in her loving support. Thanks, babe!

Have something you want to chat about after reading the book? Let us know what worked and what didn't. We value your feedback. Seriously. You make us better!

- Leave a message on our Facebook Wall: http://facebook.com/youthministry360
- Shoot us an email at feedback@youthministry360.com
- Or give us a call, 1-888-96-ym360